IDEAS FOR PE GAMES

BATH SPA UNIVERSITY

KS2

P4 to 7

AUTHOR
Elizabeth Pike

DESIGNER
Sarah Rock

EDITOR
Alison Rosier

ILLUSTRATIONS
Bethan Matthews

ASSISTANT EDITOR
Dulcie Booth

COVER ARTWORK
Andy Parker

SERIES DESIGNER
Anna Oliwa

Text © 2001 Elizabeth Pike
© 2001 Scholastic Ltd

Designed using Adobe Pagemaker
Published by Scholastic Ltd, Villiers House, Clarendon
Avenue, Leamington Spa, Warwickshire CV32 5PR

567890   567890

British Library Cataloguing-in-Publication Data
A catalogue record for this book is available from the
British Library.

ISBN 0-439-01826-9

Contents

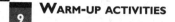

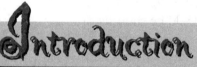

Introduction

Most 7–11 year olds react with energy and enthusiasm to any physical activity and it is for this reason that this age group is well suited to consolidating games skills already learned and learning new ones. They are ready to take a very active part in team activities where co-operation and communication can be well utilized. The effective teaching of games in physical education will also encourage self-discipline and release energies in a controlled manner, often enhancing self-esteem.

THE VALUE OF FITNESS

As people are relying more and more on the use of the car and as activities such as watching television and playing on the computer are becoming major leisure activities for children of all ages, the place and value of general body fitness is of paramount importance. Consistent teaching of games, with children regularly being given tasks that raise their pulse and heart rate, is therefore vital in education.

SELF-ESTEEM

Many children who have a low self-esteem can benefit greatly from games lessons. Tasks can usually be differentiated quite readily and easily in a lesson so that every child, whatever their physical ability, should feel they can achieve something worthwhile.

Apart from learning new physical skills, children can feel a great sense of well-being after a lesson that has combined skill with hard physical running or other moving activities. Children with behavioural problems in the classroom frequently exhibit improved behaviour when their energies are directed in physical activities.

WHAT TO WEAR

Many schools have a dress code for PE lessons but if there isn't one in your school, children should be asked to dress appropriately and, very importantly, safely. For warm weather, or when the children have been properly warmed up by relevant activities, a T-shirt or polo shirt with a pair of loose-fitting shorts, or a short games skirt for girls, to allow ease of movement, is ideal. Children should always be encouraged to wear socks even on very hot days because they stop the feet and toes slipping around inside the shoes. During cold spells of winter weather, children should be encouraged to wear a sweatshirt over their T-shirt and, if necessary, bring in comfortable trousers such as jogging bottoms to wear during the warm-up to the lesson. If the children are then sufficiently warm, you can tell them to remove the extra clothing for the remainder of the lesson. However, it is important that any child who is cold, especially those of slight build, should be allowed to keep on extra clothing for a longer period of time. This will ensure that the children enjoy the lesson and that their muscles remain warm.

Shoes should be plimsolls, if possible, but if trainers are allowed, they should be of the flexible variety that allow children to stand and move comfortably on the balls of their feet. Older children will soon begin asking to wear football boots. Safety considerations dictate that groups of children wearing plimsolls should not be playing games in the same groups as those who are wearing football boots.

Jewellery should be taken off for the games lesson but problems do arise when children have recently had ears pierced or cannot take off a ring because it is too tight. Problems such as these can be overcome by putting lightweight surgical tape over ear-rings or sharp rings during games lessons. Long hair should be tied back.

THE WARM-UP

It is very important that children who take part in physical exertion should be thoroughly warmed up before they have to move at full speed. The purpose of the warm-up is threefold. First, the muscles are stretched and gradually worked at greater speeds so that they are ready for full speed activities. Secondly, the joints are loosened and moved in all directions ready for full movement and thirdly, the hand and eye are used in certain activities so that co-ordination is at its peak for tasks using balls and other equipment.

Children should be set tasks from 'Warm-up activities' (Section 1) to ensure that all the body parts are ready. A minimum of three or four of these activities should be used at the beginning of the lesson.

REGULAR USE OF SKILLS

Although children enjoy playing games in groups, this will not work successfully unless they have developed the skills to use in the various games. Skills should be practised regularly in very small groups, or as an individual, so that they can be used to some purpose in mini-games.

Skills can be taught in several ways. You can decide at the beginning of a half-term or term to concentrate on a set of skills from one group of games, choosing one to two on which to concentrate. Alternatively, you could decide to concentrate on particular skills such as throwing and catching which will eventually be used in a variety of mini-games. You could also decide to concentrate on invasion or net skills for a term (see 'Summer/winter games' below). Planning should always be done with consistency in mind.

It is sometimes necessary to stop a group games activity and practise a particular skill, or make a mental note of the skill needed and do some work on it the following lesson. The value of practising a set number of skills in one term or half-term is that children will more readily introduce it into their group games sessions.

PRAISE

During the course of the games lesson, praise should be used extensively. Children will give 100 per cent effort when they know that the teacher is watching them work and rewarding their efforts by positive comments which may be said quietly or called out across the playing area. Wrong movements can be quietly corrected by individual teaching as you move around the class.

COPING WITH LEFT-HANDEDNESS

Most classes will have one or more left-handers in them. If children are to learn correct techniques, it is essential that every activity is shown to the class with both left- and right-handed body positions. This can be done both verbally and with physical demonstration. It will quickly become second nature to show or call out 'right foot back with right hand' or 'left foot back with left hand'.

CHILDREN WITH PHYSICAL DISABILITIES

Many children with a variety of physical disabilities now take a full and active part in games lessons. All of the activities in this book can be broken down into smaller segments so that a child with a disability can do some part of every activity. For example, a child in a wheelchair can be taught to throw a ball underarm or overarm without the mention of how the feet might be placed. All the children in a class should regularly be encouraged to work as a partner or in a group with a child who has a disability.

TEACHER DEMONSTRATION

There are a number of reasons to use demonstration in the lesson. It is often quicker to show an activity rather than explain it and some children learn more quickly if they are shown what to do rather than have to sit and listen to an explanation. A class regularly needs to see a good role model doing some of the tasks that they will

attempt. It is not necessary for your personal standard to be high, only that you can demonstrate the correct stance or action. After a session of hard running it can be a useful way of resting children's bodies whilst keeping their attention on the task at hand.

If you are going to give the children a teaching point then it is fine to stop everyone and make the point loudly. However, much of the talking you do will involve more than a teaching point and it is essential that the class is trained to move towards you and stand still on your command. Good use can be made of lines on the playground or field so that children know where they are to come up to and stand in order to see and hear clearly. It is helpful if children are used to working in set pairs before they go outside. It saves time and gives order to the way they will stand in front of you.

INTERCHANGING EQUIPMENT

Lack of adequate equipment may present some initial problems to the class teacher. Warming-up activities and skill practices need a good supply of balls, bats and other small equipment.

However, if these pieces of equipment are in short supply, it is still possible to cover all the areas of the lesson. Some tasks do not require each child to have the same sized ball so different sizes can be utilized. If bats are not readily available in sufficient quantities, tasks can be given to groups of three or four as opposed to two children. The hand is a very useful substitute for the bat and half the class can do the set task with a bat and the other half can use their hand before changing over to give everyone a chance to use both options. If there are no nets available, two benches from the school hall or gym can be stacked with the two wide surfaces together to create a workable obstacle. Another alternative would be to chalk a line or place a rope on the ground for children to hit a ball over.

Where a moving task is set using a piece of equipment, the class can be split into two or more groups and take it in turns to complete the activity.

STRUCTURE OF THE LESSON

It is tempting on a hot summer's day to do a quick warm-up activity and then proceed to the skill section. It is important that both teacher and children understand the importance of a proper warm-up because however warm the child feels, this may not be the same as having warm muscles and joints or accurate hand-eye co-ordination.

After the warm-up the children should be given tasks individually or in pairs where they can improve or learn new techniques. The class can then be given tasks involving larger group activity which will often incorporate mini-games based on skills they will need at a later stage, or smaller versions of known games. Children should also be given experience in making rules and games from their own imagination (see 'Creative games' on page 52).

Lastly, but equally important, the class should be given one or two warming-down activities that will calm them and prepare them for more sedentary work. These can take the form of gymnastic-type stretching exercises or warming-up exercises can be used as long as they are done slowly and with control.

ENHANCING LISTENING SKILLS

Owing to the nature of the environment in which the outdoor games lesson will take place, enabling the children to hear you and make them aware of your intentions for them may raise a variety of problems.

Children need to be taught simple strategies for coming to attention so that they can listen to you. A whistle is a useful addition to your personal equipment and one short blast is usually enough to bring the class to attention. If you prefer, you can use the method of raising a hand in the air and asking all children to raise their hand when they are looking and listening. This should always be done quickly so that muscles and joints don't get cold and, if the weather is at all windy, allowances need to be made so that children can hear and understand well.

ENDING THE LESSON

At the end of a games lesson when children are working at full capacity, it is important to cool down the body and mentally prepare the children for sedentary activities. Both these aims are achieved by spending a few minutes doing tasks which can be selected from the warming-up section, or doing some stretching exercises using gymnastic movement. An additional advantage to these tasks is that the class is brought together to work as one and the lesson is ended with control and discipline.

ADVERSE WEATHER

If the correct clothing for games lessons in the winter months is worn, there is no reason why lessons should not take place out of doors for most of the year.
If the weather is very cold and the children are younger, the warming-up part of the lesson could take place indoors and children could then go outside for the remainder of the session.

If you experience a bout of bad weather but still want the class to go outside, then write out the group activities on paper and let the children read them before they go outside. If they are aware of the nature of some of the work, it will mean less standing and listening in the cold or wet.

If the weather means that the games lesson is taken indoors, the tasks given may need to be adjusted but the sections of the lesson can still be taught. If the hall is small, children can be put into pairs and take it in turns to practise the tasks. When children are working in pairs, they should all be facing in two directions only as opposed to facing in directions of choice. Where possible, sponge balls should be used and the hand can be used effectively as a bat.

SUMMER/WINTER GAMES

Children at the top of the Key Stage 2 range will be familiar with the names of the major games and will be regularly playing them in mini versions as well as occasionally in their full version.

Whilst it has become increasingly popular to play football all the year round, it is important educationally that children get a chance to experience all the games in equal proportion. One of the advantages to the child of experiencing as many major games in summer and winter as possible, is that they have a choice of activities which may become lifelong leisure pursuits. Hockey, netball and football will therefore mainly be given time in the winter months with tennis, cricket, rounders and athletics being given priority in the summer months. Variations on major games such as shinty and short tennis can be incorporated as necessary.

HOW THE ACTIVITIES ARE ORGANIZED

To speed up planning and make for easy reference, all the warm-up activities are in Section 1. Sections 2, 3 and 4 give activities for invasion games, striking and fielding games and net and wall games. Each of these sections is subdivided into activities which need one or two players and activities, including mini-games, which need larger groups. Mini-games are dealt with in more detail in section 5.

Ideally, each games lesson should comprise a warm-up, a skills section followed by a mini-game session, and finally a warming-down activity. With good organization and careful planning, it is possible to do all these things within a half-hour lesson so that each week the children have a balanced lesson whether it is inside the school hall or outside on the playground or field. However, if two short sessions are available each week, you may wish to spread these activities so that the mini-game session takes up most of one lesson. If this is the case, it is important that children are warmed up and warmed down properly in each lesson (see Section 1). The skills activities can be taught during the one lesson and the mini-game during the following lesson.

The photocopiable pages at the end of this book can be used in two ways. Some of them can be used as an extra resource in science activities. They will also stand alone and can be used as a theory lesson specifically for PE. Some of the pages can be used as an ongoing activity running parallel to the practical lessons, for example the three progress charts.

Finally, the skills grid on page 64 will ensure that if you are planning a term's work with specific skills in mind, you will find the pages noted for easy reference.

WARM-UP ACTIVITIES

The activities in this section may be used in any order. Use them at the beginning of a lesson as a warm-up, or at the end as warming-down exercises. When warming up, it is not always necessary to begin with a task that involves a lot of running. Running tasks are best spaced evenly during the warm-up so that the children can start slowly and build up to full speed.

The activities in this section focus on:
- using a variety of equipment
- moving in different directions
- moving at different speeds
- rolling, throwing and bouncing exercises
- co-operating with other children
- using the available space.

WHISTLE AND RUN

RESOURCES AND CLASS MANAGEMENT
Children work as a whole class following your instructions. If you prefer, you can use a whistle instead of a voice command. Copies of photocopiable page 54 for each child are optional.

WHAT TO DO
Tell the children to go and stand in a space and face you. Tell them that at all times during the activity they must remain facing you even when moving in different directions. Explain that you will point with your arm and hand in a direction that can be right, left, in front or behind your body, at the same time shouting 'Go', or if you have a whistle you can blow a short blast. Tell the children that when they see in which direction you are pointing, they are to run as fast as possible in that direction. Do not keep them running in one direction for very long. As soon as they have taken a few short running steps, point in another direction and blow the whistle or shout.

Make sure that the children start the activity on the balls of their feet and keep the body weight forward so that they are well balanced. Make sure that the children realize that the object is to take short steps in order to run as quickly as possible. When they are experienced at this activity, try pointing in the same direction on two or more occasions before changing to another direction.

'My warm-up chart' on photocopiable page 54 at the end of this book may be used with the children to reinforce the importance of warming up the legs.

DIFFERENTIATION
Some children may find the speed at which you point in a new direction too fast for them to react to quickly enough. If this happens you can slow down your commands although this will inevitably lead to children running slightly slower. When children have been practising this activity for some time or when they are thoroughly warmed up, the commands should be speeded up so that they can change direction more frequently.

NOW OR LATER
To follow this activity with a similar one that needs short, quick steps, tell the children to find a partner and stand one behind the other. At your command, the child standing behind should run a short distance to the right then quickly to the left and

OBJECTIVES
To enable children to:
- change direction with speed
- follow quick-fire instructions
- warm up leg muscles.

CROSS-CURRICULAR LINKS
DANCE
Responding to a range of stimuli.

GYMNASTICS
Including variations in speed and direction.

try losing their partner who has been attempting to keep pace with the changes of direction. The children can change over so that they each have a turn at attempting to shake off their partner.

ROLL AND SNATCH

OBJECTIVES
To enable children to:
- practise retrieving a ball
- practise a rolling technique
- warm up the leg muscles.

CROSS-CURRICULAR LINKS
GYMNASTICS
Creating and performing fluent sequences.

RESOURCES AND CLASS MANAGEMENT
Children work individually or in pairs. Each child will need a ball but if balls are in short supply, children can share one between two. Ideally, the ball will be large so that retrieval is made easier but different-sized balls may be used.

WHAT TO DO
Tell the children to collect a ball each and make a line across the playground or field all facing in the same direction. Right-handed children should put their right foot back and left-handed children should put their left foot back. Tell them to hold the ball with both hands either to the right or the left of their body depending on how they place their feet, then bend their knees so that as they roll the ball it will be nearer the ground. After the ball has left their hand they should run after it and use both hands to scoop up the ball and turn to run back to their original starting point. Explain that it is easier to scoop up the ball if they run ahead of it and turn to face it before trying to retrieve it.

DIFFERENTIATION
The smaller the ball, the faster it will roll, so younger or less able children should use the largest possible sized balls.

Older or more capable children can try this with smaller balls but, again, emphasize the need to run ahead of the ball and turn to face it before scooping it up.

NOW OR LATER
Organize the class so that they are working in pairs. As before, one child rolls the ball but remains standing whilst the other child runs to retrieve the ball and brings it back to the starting position.

LEFT AND RIGHT BOUNCE

OBJECTIVES
To enable children to:
- practise hand-eye co-ordination
- practise the skill of controlled bouncing
- warm up arms and shoulders.

CROSS-CURRICULAR LINKS
GYMNASTICS
Creating and performing fluent sequences.

RESOURCES AND CLASS MANAGEMENT
Children work independently in a small space. Each child will need a large or medium-sized ball. Copies of photocopiable page 54 for each child are optional.

WHAT TO DO
Tell the children to hold the ball in both hands initially. This aids ball control at the beginning of the task. Tell them they are going to let go of the ball with their right hand and, using their left hand, they are going to push the ball to the ground with some force. The hand should be as flat as possible when pushing the ball down. As the ball rises, they should push it to the ground a second time and again a third time, as it rises. Tell the children that it is important to push the ball in a straight downward line towards the ground so that they do not need to move their feet when repeating the bounces. After three bounces using the left hand, the children should repeat the action with the right hand. Encourage them to keep the sequence of left, right, left, right bouncing for as long as they can, all the time encouraging them to be accurate with their bouncing so that movement of feet is minimal.

'My warm-up chart' on photocopiable page 54 at the end of this book may be used with the children to reinforce the importance of warming up the arms and shoulders.

DIFFERENTIATION
Smaller balls may be used by older children but it is important that they are shown a different technique for the bouncing action. When using a small ball, the hand should be placed around the ball as it is pushed to the ground and not kept flat. Children should also be aware that they can control the height at which the ball bounces by the degree of force they use to push it down.

NOW OR LATER
When the children have some degree of control and can keep the left, right sequence going for some time, set them the task of making the degree of bounce either higher or lower. Let them experiment with the amount of effort and push it takes to make the ball go higher and lower. When they have done this you can set tasks which require them to do three low bounces with each hand followed by three high bounces.

FOLLOW MY LEADER CHANGE

RESOURCES AND CLASS MANAGEMENT
Children work in groups of four. Copies of photocopiable page 58 for each child are optional.

WHAT TO DO
Ask the children to find a partner and then go and join up with another pair. Tell them to stand one behind the other. The leader may face in any direction but must have a clear space in front of them to begin running. Tell the leader of each of the groups that he/she will begin running slowly anywhere in the area and the remainder of the group are to follow the leader but they must keep in the place and the line that they started in. The children should be made aware that the activity becomes too difficult if the leader runs too fast. After the children have begun to jog slowly, you will shout 'Go' and on that command, the children at the back of each group should increase their running speed, run past the front three children and move to the front to become the new leader. When the groups have settled into a slow jogging mode with the new leader, repeat the 'Go' command for the new rear children to sprint to the front of their line.

It may be appropriate for children to use 'My fitness record' on photocopiable page 58 to investigate the effect of exercise on their pulse rates.

OBJECTIVES
To enable children to:
■ work co-operatively with a group of children
■ warm up the leg muscles and shoulder joints
■ practise moving in different directions whilst in motion.

CROSS-CURRICULAR LINKS
SCIENCE
Investigating the effect of exercise and rest on pulse rate.

DIFFERENTIATION

Younger or less able children may find a group of four too many to overtake, in which case the groups can be reduced to three or even two to begin the practice.

Older and more able children should be able to operate in groups of five or six but this may reduce the time they will be able to practise the activity.

NOW OR LATER

When starting this activity, especially if it is used as the first practice of the lesson, you should make sure there are long gaps between your commands so that the children do not have to sprint too much. However, when they are well warmed up and if the children are older, you can increase the number of times you shout the command 'Go'. This will increase the number of times that each child reaches the rear of the group and therefore has to sprint to the front.

BODY BOUNCE

OBJECTIVES

To enable children to:
■ practise ball control
■ become more aware of their bodies
■ warm up joints.

CROSS-CURRICULAR LINKS

PSHE

Understanding the importance of a healthy diet.

GYMNASTICS

Including variations in level, speed and direction in sequences.

RESOURCES AND CLASS MANAGEMENT

Children work independently or in pairs. Each child will need a large ball. This activity can also be done with children working independently but sharing a ball with a partner. The children work with a small amount of space around their entire body. Copies of photocopiable pages 54 and 59 for each child are optional.

WHAT TO DO

Tell the children to begin by holding the ball in both hands at about waist height. They should lift one leg with the knee bent and drop the ball on top of the thigh close to the knee joint. As the ball makes contact with the leg, tell the children to push upwards with the bent leg so that the ball bounces off and into the air. When the ball is in the air, tell the children to bend an arm and push the arm upwards underneath the ball so that it bounces off their forearm. You can then tell them to try pushing the ball back into the air with different parts of their bodies. At first the children may try unsuitable parts of the body such as the back or stomach but you can encourage them to use the top of the ankle between the shin and the foot as well as the top of their legs.

The children should be aware that they may have to move from the spot where they began the task as the ball will not necessarily go upwards in a straight line.

'My warm-up chart' on photocopiable page 54 at the end of this book may be used with the children to reinforce the importance of warming up the different parts of the body.

DIFFERENTIATION

Younger or less able children will find this task easier if you suggest one or two of the easier parts of the body to them to use, for example the foot or knee.

Older children can try to repeatedly bounce the ball off one part of the body as many times as they can.

NOW OR LATER

■ This activity can be performed in pairs. Tell the pairs of children to stand facing each other at a distance of about four strides. One child drops the ball onto a part of their body and bounces it off in the direction of their partner. The partner moves quickly whilst the ball is in the air and either catches it and then bounces it off a part of the body or bounces it straight back without catching it.

■ To reinforce learning about the importance of a healthy diet, you may wish to ask children to complete photocopiable page 59 ('Food for fitness') back in the classroom after the lesson.

COUNT AND THROW

RESOURCES AND CLASS MANAGEMENT
Children work in pairs. Each pair will need one ball between them. Copies of photocopiable page 58 for each child are optional.

WHAT TO DO
Tell each pair to collect a ball and go and stand in a space facing each other. They should have enough room to stand three or four strides apart. It is safer if you have all children facing in two directions only to prevent children from colliding with each other when retrieving balls that have gone astray.

Explain that the child holding the ball should hold it at chest height, close to the chest with their hands behind and slightly to the side of the ball and with their fingers spread and thumbs pointing downwards. The front leg should be slightly bent. They must push the ball in a straight line towards their partner. The child catching the ball should reach up slightly higher than their chest, with their arms outstretched to receive the ball and bring it in to their chest. Again, this child will have their front leg slightly bent and should

OBJECTIVES
To enable children to:
■ practise throwing and catching skills
■ focus on throwing at speed
■ warm up hand-eye co-ordination.

CROSS-CURRICULAR LINKS
ATHLETICS
Participating in challenges that call for precision, speed, power and stamina.

SCIENCE
Investigating the effect of exercise on pulse and heart rate.

return the ball with a similar chest pass. Ask the children to count each throw. This continues until you decide to blow the whistle and stop the practice. Ask each pair of children how many throws they managed in the time you gave them.

Make sure the children know that the idea of the practice is to make as many short quick throws as possible. There should be a competitive element in this practice and you can begin by telling the children that you will let them throw for two minutes before you blow the whistle.

It may be appropriate for children to use 'My fitness record' on photocopiable page 58 to investigate the effect of exercise on their pulse rates.

DIFFERENTIATION
Older children can vary the type of passes they do. For example, they could do overarm passes or bounce passes. However, the children should be aware that chest passes are the quickest.

If young children find the chest pass more difficult, an overarm or underarm pass can be used.

NOW OR LATER
When the children are proficient in this practice, you can give them a sequence of passes that they must adhere to whilst they are counting, for example chest pass, underarm pass, overarm pass, bounce pass. This makes them really think hard about the passing as well as the number of passes.

TOUCH HOME

OBJECTIVES

To enable children to:
■ increase speed whilst running
■ warm up all body parts
■ increase awareness of space.

CROSS-CURRICULAR LINKS
PSHE

Understanding the importance of a healthy diet.

RESOURCES AND CLASS MANAGEMENT

Children work independently. Copies of photocopiable page 59 for each child are optional (for 'Now or later' activity).

WHAT TO DO

The children should begin by standing in a space and facing a direction ahead where they will have enough room to run forward. Tell the children that when you blow a whistle or shout they should run slowly forward taking steps to avoid colliding with anyone else in the class. On hearing the next whistle blast, they should bend their knees, pause and touch the ground with a hand, before rising and running slowly ahead again. In order to properly warm up the body, you should emphasize that the running should be slow. Speed can be gradually increased but the children should not be encouraged to sprint really fast as they will need maximum control when they pause and touch the ground.

DIFFERENTIATION

If less able children find it difficult to bend their knees and touch the ground after pausing, they can be told to stop and stand very still until you blow the whistle again.

NOW OR LATER

■ Practising changing direction can be introduced into this activity quite easily. Tell the children that as soon as they have touched the ground on the first occasion, they should quickly turn and face a new direction before moving off. Encourage them to run with short steps as this will give them better control over their bodies as they pause and touch the ground.
■ To reinforce learning about the importance of a healthy diet, you may wish to ask children to complete photocopiable page 59 ('Food for fitness') back in the classroom.

UP AND DOWN

OBJECTIVES

To enable children to:
■ practise throwing skills
■ practise catching and retrieving skills
■ warm up hand-eye co-ordination.

CROSS-CURRICULAR LINKS
GYMNASTICS

Creating and performing fluent sequences.

ATHLETICS

Pacing themselves in challenges and competitions.

RESOURCES AND CLASS MANAGEMENT

Children work independently. Each child will need access to a ball which may be of any size.

WHAT TO DO

Children should be standing in their own space with some space around their body to allow for a small amount of movement. Tell the children to hold the ball in one or both hands depending on its size, and to hold it at chest level. Tell them to throw the ball upwards in as straight a line as possible. The ball should go higher than the head but should not be thrown excessively high. When the ball is in the air, they should reach upwards with both hands, fingers spread. As they make contact with the ball, they should pull it in towards the stomach. Encourage the children to focus attention on throwing the ball up in as direct a pathway as possible. They should not

14

have to move their feet very much if they perform the task correctly. When the children repeat this task they should aim to try and keep the movements continuous so that there is no gap between catching the ball and throwing it upwards.

DIFFERENTIATION

If there is a wall or high fence readily available, tell the children to throw the ball in a straight line and underarm to a point on the wall or fence which is higher than their head. As they catch the rebound, encourage them to reach out with their arms and hands, fingers apart, to catch the ball and bring it into their body.

NOW OR LATER

When the children are familiar with this activity, you can introduce an element of competition by asking them to count the number of throws they can make in a given time. Points can be deducted if they drop the ball and have to retrieve it. Although they will adjust their throwing to achieve as many as possible, make sure they still throw above the head each time.

LOSE YOUR PARTNER

RESOURCES AND CLASS MANAGEMENT

Children work in pairs and the children in each pair should be numbered 1 and 2. Copies of photocopiable page 54 for each child are optional.

WHAT TO DO

Tell the children to stand together in a space with number 1 standing in front of number 2. They should both be facing in the same direction so that number 1 is looking over their right or left shoulder to see what number 2 is doing and copy them. Number 2 is going to use very short, quick steps sideways to draw number 1 with him/her and then very quickly run in the opposite direction leaving number 1 to move in the original direction. The children should be aware that it may take them several feint runs in each of the sideways directions before they run quickly to lose their partner. You should also explain that it is not always necessary to move the body and the feet to one side – it is equally efficient to move the top of the body to one side then the other before moving the feet and running. It is tempting for some children who can run fast to keep running long distances in an effort to lose their partner. This should be discouraged. The idea is to trick the other child into thinking that they are going to move in one direction but then go in another. 'My warm-up chart' on photocopiable page 54 at the end of this book may be used with the children to reinforce the importance of warming up the legs.

DIFFERENTIATION

If less able children find this difficult, give them a short sequence to follow, for example, feint to the left, feint to the right, feint to the left then run to the right. This may mean that their partner will be able to stay with them but it will give them a structure to follow and will mean they can learn the dodging technique.

NOW OR LATER

When children are confident that they can lose a partner quickly, they can be taught how to signal to another player that they are ready to receive a ball. Number 2 feints and dodges as before and when they have run quickly and are free of their partner they should raise one hand in the air with the arm straight. If they are moving to the right, the right hand is raised and if they are moving to the left, then the left hand should be raised. Discourage children from calling out at the same time. Explain that in a games situation they may wish their team players to know they are available to receive the ball but will not wish to draw attention to the opposite team.

OBJECTIVES
To enable children to:
■ practise dodging skills
■ work co-operatively
■ warm up the feet and legs.

CROSS-CURRICULAR LINKS
GYMNASTICS
Including variations in speed, level and direction.

TWO BALL CATCH

To enable children to:
■ improve hand-eye co-ordination
■ work co-operatively
■ warm up arm and shoulder muscles and joints.

RESOURCES AND CLASS MANAGEMENT

Children work in pairs. Every child will need a ball. The balls may vary in size but it is important that the two balls used by each pair of children are the same size.

WHAT TO DO

Tell the children to find a space and face each other a short distance apart. Tell them that they should hold the ball at chest height with fingers spread at the back of the ball and thumbs pointing downwards as they are going to use a chest pass to throw. Explain that chest throws are ideal for making short, quick passes. If any children are using small balls, they should hold it in one hand only and throw underarm. Emphasize that right-handers should have the right foot back and left-handers the left foot back. The arm should be swung backwards and as it comes forward, the ball should be released at about waist height.

Tell the children that they are going to watch their partner very closely and both throw the ball to each other at the same time. Immediately they have thrown their ball they must be ready to catch the ball which was thrown by their partner. Encourage them to keep going unless the ball is not caught and has to be retrieved. If the balls collide in mid-air, encourage the children to agree that one of them should throw slightly higher than chest height next time to avoid it happening again.

DIFFERENTIATION

Younger or less able children should use larger balls and will find it easier if they throw underarm.

Older and more able children can try counting the number of passes they throw and catch and try and improve their record.

NOW OR LATER

When children are confident and have gained some success with this practice, you can ask them to alternate chest and bounce passes. Tell the children to number themselves 1 and 2. Number 1 throws a chest pass whilst number 2 does a bounce pass by pushing the ball down to the ground at about the centre point between themselves and their partner. Number 1 then does a bounce pass whilst number 2 does a chest pass. This can be continued until the children can do it several times.

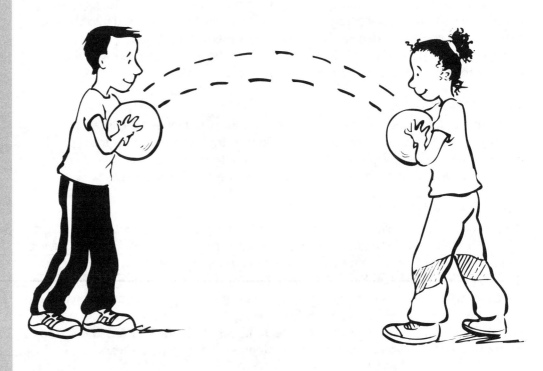

The activities in this section cover tasks and skills relevant in hockey, netball and football. As these are considered major games, the skills and group activities associated with them need to be practised regularly throughout the autumn and spring terms.

The activities in this section focus on:
- using a variety of methods to pass a ball
- practising shooting techniques
- working co-operatively with another person
- using the space to move, dodge and pass
- using obstacles to improve skills
- introducing hockey skills.

DRIBBLE ME ROUND

RESOURCES AND CLASS MANAGEMENT

Children work in pairs. Each pair will need one large ball between them.

WHAT TO DO

Ask the children to face their partners with eight paces between them. Tell the children with a ball to place it on the ground in front of them. Tell them to move forward and, at the same time, dribble the ball tapping it from one foot to the other as they move. Several taps may be made with one foot before pushing the ball to the other foot. Emphasize that the ball should never be more than a few centimetres from the feet so that it is always under control. As the children with the balls move forward, they should dribble the ball to either the left or right side of their partners, who remain standing still. The ball should then be dribbled around the back of the stationary children and back to the original starting position. The players with the ball should then turn to face their partner and kick the ball to them. It may be necessary for the children with a ball to trap it by placing a foot lightly on it before they kick to a partner. Emphasize that the ball should only be kicked hard enough for it to arrive at their partner's feet.

The children receiving the balls should then move forward, dribbling the ball towards their partner in the same way as before. Explain to the children that they should try and keep the movements flowing with no big pauses between the dribbling and the kicking.

OBJECTIVES
To enable children to:
- practise the skill of dribbling a ball
- improve accurate passing
- work co-operatively.

CROSS-CURRICULAR LINKS
GYMNASTICS
Creating and performing fluent sequences.

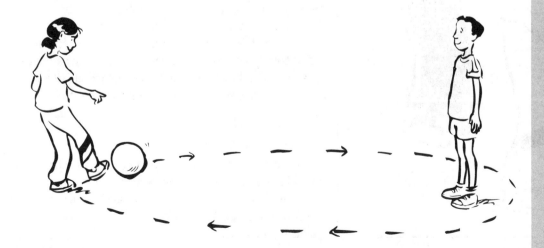

DIFFERENTIATION

Younger children could begin by dribbling the ball around a partner and as they reach the side of them, they tap the ball to them and run back to the original starting place. The child with the ball then dribbles it towards their partner and repeats the movements.

Older or more able children can be encouraged to increase speed as they dribble the ball forward.

NOW OR LATER

When the children become accurate with their passing skills they can be encouraged to turn after dribbling the ball and kick it into the space to the left or right of their partner. Their partner should then anticipate and runs towards the ball before trapping it and dribbling it back to their partner.

DODGE DUO

OBJECTIVES

To enable children to:
■ practise the skill of dodging
■ use space economically
■ learn how to signal silently to other players.

RESOURCES AND CLASS MANAGEMENT

Children work in pairs. They will need no equipment but should have some space to use all around them.

WHAT TO DO

Tell the children to number themselves 1 and 2 in their pairs. Number 1 stands in front of number 2 and they both face in the same direction. Number 1 looks over their right or left shoulder so that they can see number 2. Make number 1 aware that they must follow number 2 wherever they go. Number 2 moves the top part of the body quickly to the right without moving feet, then quickly to the left without moving feet. At this point number 2 can decide to repeat the movements or can quickly sprint to the right to try and lose number 1. When number 2 is several paces ahead of number 1, they should raise the right hand and arm high to signal to an imaginary player that they are available to receive a pass.

Ask the children to change over so that number 1 is behind and tries to lose number 2. Emphasize that the faster the children make the body movements, the more likely they are to fool their partner into thinking they are going to run in that direction.

DIFFERENTIATION

Less able children who find the feinting movements with the top part of the body difficult, can be encouraged to run a few short steps instead.

More able children can be encouraged to see how quickly and in how small a space they can lose their partner. In other words, discourage children from using superior speed to outdistance their partner.

NOW OR LATER

When the children are familiar with this practice, introduce a competitive element by telling them that the first person to put up a hand to signal gains a point. See how many points they have gained after a number of tries.

DRIBBLE AND PUSH

RESOURCES AND CLASS MANAGEMENT

You will need hockey or shinty sticks, some rubber balls and some skittles or other obstacles. Depending on the amount of equipment you have available, the children should work in pairs with two sticks, one ball and one obstacle between them. Copies of photocopiable page 55 for each child are optional.

WHAT TO DO

Tell the children to place the obstacle on the ground, some distance from them and stand one behind the other facing it. Tell the children they are going to dribble the ball towards and around the obstacle. Ask the children who are in front to place the ball on the ground in front of them. Tell them to hold the stick so that the left hand is at the top of the stick and the right hand is halfway down the stick. The stick should be held at the right side of the body. Keeping the stick close to the ground, tell the children they must tap the ball lightly so that it moves but does not go too far ahead. They must run slowly and keep tapping the ball until they reach the obstacle. Then, keeping the obstacle to their right side, they must move around it, still tapping the ball lightly every few seconds. As they circle the obstacle and face their partner, tell the children that they should push the ball hard with their stick towards their partner who is waiting. Their partner must stop the ball with the stick then proceed to tap it towards the obstacle before repeating the actions of their partner.

DIFFERENTIATION

Younger children may be told to tap the ball around the obstacle and then return to their places without pushing the ball to a partner. At a later stage they can practise pushing the ball to a partner before combining the two actions.

Older or more able children can be encouraged to travel faster whilst they are dribbling the ball.

NOW OR LATER

When children can carry out this activity with some skill, you can add one or more extra obstacles so that they are travelling in a figure of eight as they dribble the ball before pushing it back to their partner. You could use 'My progress chart 1' on photocopiable page 55 for children to record how many times they manage to complete a figure of eight.

OBJECTIVES

To enable children to:
■ practise using sticks to move the ball
■ practise manoeuvring around an obstacle
■ practise a push pass.

CROSS-CURRICULAR LINKS

GYMNASTICS
Including variations in level, speed and direction.

BLOCK THE BALL

OBJECTIVES
To enable children to:
- practise blocking tactics
- practise dribbling skills
- use dodging tactics.

CROSS-CURRICULAR LINKS
ATHLETICS
Pacing themselves in challenges and competitions.

RESOURCES AND CLASS MANAGEMENT
Children work in pairs. Each pair will need one large ball between them.

WHAT TO DO
Children should find a partner and number themselves 1 and 2. Ask each pair to fetch one ball between them and find a space in which to work. Ask child number 1 of each pair to stand with the ball on the ground in front of their feet. Tell number 2 to walk several long strides away from their partner, then turn to face them. Explain to the children with the ball (number 1) that they should dribble the ball by tapping it with one or alternate feet using the top or the inside of the foot, towards number 2. Number 2 must stand still until number 1 is quite close, then number 1 must move in front of the ball whilst number 2 tries to dribble to the right or left in an attempt to avoid number 1. Make sure the children understand that at this stage they are not to try and win the ball away from their partner – the idea is that they move in front of their partner, making them move to one side or the other. If number 1 manages to avoid number 2's blocking manoeuvre, they should then, after a short dribbling move, pass the ball to number 2 and go and stand opposite waiting for their turn to block the ball.

DIFFERENTIATION
Older or more able children can soon be encouraged to try and win the ball by moving towards their partner and tackling before number 1 tries to move left or right.

Younger children can try this activity without using a ball at first. Number 1 runs towards number 2 and as number 2 comes nearer and tries to move left or right, number 1 should try to move sideways and block the move. Make sure the children understand that they must not come into contact with their partner and that they must remain facing them.

NOW OR LATER
As children become more expert at this practice, they can be taught a dodging tactic involving moving the ball one way whilst they run another. As number 1 dribbles the ball and moves nearer to number 2, they should give the ball a light tap to the left of their partner whilst running to the right of their partner with the intention of retrieving the ball as they leave their partner behind.

This activity can also be done using hockey sticks or shinty sticks. If tackling is encouraged, then each child must have a stick. If the children are only going to practise blocking their partner, then only the children with the ball need a stick.

THROW AND BOUNCE

OBJECTIVES
To enable children to:
- work co-operatively
- practise throwing and bouncing skills
- practise receiving the ball from a variety of passes.

RESOURCES AND CLASS MANAGEMENT
Children work in pairs. Each pair will need one large ball between them.

WHAT TO DO
Tell the children to collect a ball and stand facing their partner with five paces between them. Explain that they are going to throw the ball to their partner who, in turn, will bounce it back to them.

To throw the ball, children should hold it in their preferred hand, just in front of the shoulder on the same side. The hand should be placed just behind the ball. (If necessary, children with small hands can use the free hand to support the ball in front as they throw.) The body should be slightly facing the preferred side. Right-handed children should put their right foot back and left-handed children should put their left foot back. Tell the children that before they release the ball, their weight should be on the back foot. As they push the ball firmly in a straight line to their partner, the body weight should come forward onto the front foot.

To receive the ball, children should reach forward with outstretched arms and hands and fingers spread. As the ball touches their hands, tell them to pull the ball towards the chest and stomach. They should then look at a point on the ground about halfway between themselves and their partner and push the ball hard, using both hands, towards that spot so that they do a bounce pass back to their partner. As the ball rises, their partner should stretch out arms and hands to receive it and bring it into their body as before.

Finally, point out to the children that when they change over so that the other child does the overarm throw, they will be receiving the ball at a different height and must adjust accordingly. Regularly remind the children to watch the ball from the moment it leaves their partner to the time they receive it.

DIFFERENTIATION

More able children can use a chest pass instead of an overarm throw. This has the advantage of speeding up the throwing and receiving. The children will need to move closer and hold the ball at chest level with hands spread behind the ball and one foot in front of the other. Their body weight should be on the back foot. As the ball is pushed firmly and quickly towards their partner, the weight should come forward onto the front foot. Encourage children to build up speed as they do this practice.

NOW OR LATER

Vary this practice by introducing a sequence of throwing, for example, overarm throw, overarm throw, overarm throw, bounce pass, bounce pass, bounce pass. Repeat several times.

SHOOT AND THROW

RESOURCES AND CLASS MANAGEMENT

Children work in pairs. Each pair will need one large ball and some equipment to use as a shooting target. Possibilities include netball posts, basketball nets on a wall, skittles standing upright, hoops lying flat on the ground. The targets need to be spaced out in the available area so that children have as much room as possible in which to practise. You will need a stopwatch with a second hand. Copies of photocopiable page 55 for each child are optional.

WHAT TO DO

Ask each pair of children to number themselves 1 and 2. Number 1 should have a large ball and stand approximately five strides away from the target. Explain that they are going to aim and shoot at a target, retrieve the ball and throw overarm to number 2 who then has a go. If the children are shooting into high nets, tell them to stand with feet slightly apart with their preferred foot in front. Tell them to lift the ball to face height and hold it with their preferred hand behind and the other hand in front of the ball. From that position tell them to throw the ball towards the net with

CROSS-CURRICULAR LINKS
MATHEMATICS
Using pattern and relationships.

GYMNASTICS
Including variation in level and speed.

OBJECTIVES
To enable children to:
■ practise aiming and shooting skills
■ practise retrieving a ball
■ practise overarm throwing to a partner.

CROSS-CURRICULAR LINKS
GYMNASTICS
Including variation in level, speed and direction.

a lifting action which moves the ball upward as well as forward. As the ball moves towards the net, tell them to follow it and, as it falls to the floor, bend down to retrieve it. Encourage them to begin moving the feet into the correct position for an overarm throw as they scoop up the ball. As soon as the body is in the correct position for the throw, they should look towards number 2 and throw it them. Number 2 then repeats the actions.

If skittles or other targets are used for the shooting part of the practice, tell the children that the shooting action will be an underarm throw followed by retrieval and an overarm throw as in the version above.

DIFFERENTIATION

Younger or less able children can leave the ball to be retrieved by their partner. Tell number 1 to shoot at the target but as the ball hits the target, number 2 runs in and retrieves the ball before throwing it back to number 1. Number 1 can take three shots before the children change over so that number 2 shoots and number 1 retrieves.

NOW OR LATER

When the children become more accomplished at this practice, you can introduce some competition between the children. Tell them that you are going to time them for three minutes during which time they must count the number of shots that successfully go into the net or hit the target. 'My progress chart 1' on photocopiable page 55 can be used for children to record how many times they hit the target.

INVASION GAMES
GROUP ACTIVITIES FOR THREE OR MORE PLAYERS

The activities in this section focus on:
■ encouraging co-operative teamwork
■ enhancing leadership qualities
■ practising skills involving throwing, dribbling, bouncing and dodging
■ using intercepting skills to obtain the ball
■ preparing to play mini-games
■ introducing a competitive element.
The photocopiable page 'How should I behave?' on page 60 can be used in conjunction with any of these activities.

CHEST PASS SHUTTLE

OBJECTIVES

To enable children to:
■ practise the skill of using a chest pass
■ co-operate in a group situation
■ increase speed when passing the ball.

CROSS-CURRICULAR LINKS

GYMNASTICS
Including changes of speed and direction.

ATHLETICS
Throwing with accuracy.

RESOURCES AND CLASS MANAGEMENT

Children work in groups of six. Each group will need one large ball. You will also need a stopwatch with a second hand and copies of photocopiable page 55 for each child.

WHAT TO DO

Ask the children to move into groups of six and number themselves 1 to 6 within the group. Explain that numbers 1 to 3 in each group will form a line, one behind the other, with number 1 in front. The children numbered 4 to 6 also form a line, one behind the other, with number 4 facing number 1. Tell the children to check that the distance between number 1 and number 4 is no more than two long strides.

It is a good idea at this point to select one group to demonstrate under your guidance. Number 1 holds the ball at chest height with hands behind the ball and thumbs pointing downward. Elbows should be bent so that the ball is against the chest. Number 1 pushes the ball sharply and quickly to number 4, then, after releasing the ball, runs quickly to stand behind number 6. Number 4 passes with a chest pass to number 2 and, after releasing the ball, runs quickly to stand behind number 3. This continues until each group of three is once more standing in their original position. When the class have practised this at walking or slow running pace, ask them to see if they can speed up the activity by releasing the ball faster and running more quickly.

'My progress chart 1' on page 55 can be used for children to record how many times the ball is successfully passed and caught.

DIFFERENTIATION

This activity can be done in groups of four with two facing two if there are children who find working in a group of six difficult. With unequal class numbers, the groups of six can be mixed with groups of four.

For more able children, passes can be varied using alternating bounce and chest passes until the original positions have been reached.

NOW OR LATER

When children are familiar with this activity, a timed element can be introduced. For example, you can tell the class that as they throw, they should count how many passes they can achieve in one minute. This will speed up the chest passes. However, discourage the children from starting to run before they have made the pass.

SPOT YOUR NUMBER

RESOURCES AND CLASS MANAGEMENT

Children work in groups of four. Each group will need one medium-sized ball.

WHAT TO DO

Ask each group of children to form a circle by holding hands and stretching arms until they are straight. Tell them to release their hands and remain standing in that position. Ask them to number themselves 1 to 4. Tell the children with a ball to throw it upward and slightly towards the centre of their circle, at the same time calling out any of the numbers apart from their own number. As one of the children in the circle hears their number, tell them to run forward with arms and hands stretched upward to catch the ball before it falls to the ground. Explain to the children that they will have to concentrate and listen carefully so that they are ready if their number is called. When they have successfully caught the ball, tell them to return to their place in the circle and repeat the upward throw calling out another number.

DIFFERENTIATION

Younger or less able children can be told to call out a number before they throw the ball upward as this gives extra time to the child who is to catch the ball.

NOW OR LATER

When the children have practised this activity for a while, you can tell the child who catches the ball to replace the child in the circle who threw up the ball. At the same time, that child must run and stand at the point in the circle where the previous child stood.

OBJECTIVES

To enable children to:
■ increase the accuracy of throwing a ball
■ improve speed of reaction
■ to practise retrieving techniques.

LONG RUN THROWING

OBJECTIVES
To enable children to:
■ work co-operatively
■ practise overarm passing in a moving situation
■ travel with a ball.

CROSS-CURRICULAR LINKS

GYMNASTICS
Choosing and linking skills and actions in short movement phrases.

SCIENCE
Investigating the effect of exercise on pulse and heart rate.

RESOURCES AND CLASS MANAGEMENT

Children work in groups of three. This activity is suitable for throwing or kicking a ball, or using a hockey or shinty stick. If you are using it as throwing or kicking practice, you will need enough large balls (netball size for throwing and football size for kicking) for each group of children to have one between them. Children using hockey or shinty sticks will need one each and a small rubber ball for each group. Copies of photocopiable page 58 for each child are optional.

WHAT TO DO

The children start at one end of a field or playground. Each group makes a line side by side but with a space of several paces between each of them. They should all face the same way looking down the playground or field and the player at one end should be holding the ball. Tell the children that they are going to travel down the pitch or playground throwing the ball in turn to each other but explain that when they have the ball, they will be restricted in the number of steps they may take.

The player with the ball throws using an overarm pass to the player in the middle who in turn passes to the player at the far side of the group. As they take it in turns to throw, they must all run in a straight line towards the end of the pitch but making sure the distance between each of them is kept the same. The player with the ball is only allowed to take one stride and lift the back leg again before throwing it. You will need to watch carefully and correct any children who are running more than one step with the ball. If you are doing this activity with hockey or shinty sticks or

footballs, then it is preferable to tell the children that they must pass after two or three taps or kicks so that the ball is kept moving between the three children.

Finally, point out to the children that if they are in the middle of the group, they will be receiving the ball from one side and throwing it to the other and will therefore need to adjust their body position accordingly. During this practice, regularly change the player in the middle so that all three children get a turn in this position.

It may be appropriate for children to use 'My fitness record' on photocopiable page 58 to investigate the effect of exercise on their pulse rates during this activity.

DIFFERENTIATION

Younger or less able children can begin this activity by walking through it and then running slowly. Tell them that when they have the ball, they must stop and not move until they have thrown it.

NOW OR LATER

Older and more able children who are familiar with this practice can change the order of placing whilst they move. Tell the player with the ball to throw as before to the player in the centre who then passes to the player at the end. Immediately the ball has been thrown, the other two players change places as they move down the playground or field so that a new person is in the middle ready to receive the ball.

PASS, DRIBBLE AND SHOOT

RESOURCES AND CLASS MANAGEMENT

Children work in groups of three. Each group will need a large ball and use of two goalposts as a target area. If you are using goalposts on a playing field, all the children can use the same set of posts providing you line them up in groups of three so that only one group sets off at a time. If this activity is taking place on a playground or in the school hall, each group can use two skittles or other markers placed approximately five paces apart as target areas. Copies of photocopiable page 55 for each child are optional.

WHAT TO DO

Ask each group to collect a large ball and stand at least half a pitch back from the markers. Tell them to stand in a line with one at each end and a child in the middle facing the markers. The child at one end should have the ball on the ground in front of the right or left foot. On your command tell them to move forward together keeping equidistant apart. The player with the ball dribbles it by tapping it lightly with the front of the foot and then kicks it slightly ahead of the middle player so that the middle player can run onto the ball and control it by dribbling before kicking it to the player at the opposite end. This continues until the children reach a position several paces in front of the markers. Then, the player with the ball kicks it and tries to place it between the markers. One player retrieves the ball and the group runs back to their original position to begin again.

DIFFERENTIATION

Younger children may begin the initial run approximately eight metres from the markers.

Older and more able children should be encouraged to see how many passes they can make before they reach the markers. This discourages children from dribbling the ball from one end of the pitch to the other without passing it.

NOW OR LATER

At a later stage, when children are confident with this activity, they will enjoy having a fourth child to act as a goalkeeper when they shoot. Tell the goalkeepers that at this stage they are only allowed to use their feet to stop and control the ball before kicking it back, if they can, to a member of the group that is shooting. Children can use 'My progress chart 1' on photocopiable page 55 to record how many goals they score.

OBJECTIVES

To enable children to:
■ practise dribbling, kicking and shooting skills with a ball
■ work in a team situation
■ improve kicking and shooting accuracy.

CROSS-CURRICULAR LINKS
GYMNASTICS
Performing basic skills in travelling.

PIGGY IN THE MIDDLE

RESOURCES AND CLASS MANAGEMENT

Children work in groups of three. Each group will need a large ball. The balls should have maximum air in them to make the activity easier. Copies of photocopiable page 55 for each child are optional.

WHAT TO DO

Ask each group to collect a ball and stand in a line with approximately five paces between them. Player 1 at one end of the line stands holding the ball facing player 2 in the middle. Player 3 stands behind player 2 and facing his or her back. Explain that the children on the outside are going to bounce the ball to each other and the child in the middle is going to try and intercept.

Tell player 1, who is holding the ball, to stand with one foot in front and the ball

OBJECTIVES

To enable children to:
■ improve accuracy in aiming a ball
■ practise a bounce pass
■ practise intercepting a ball.

held in both hands with fingers spread at each side. They should hold the ball at chest level and look at a spot to the right of the player 2 facing them. Tell them to push the ball hard towards that spot so that it bounces by the side of the player in the middle. If correctly placed, the ball will bounce too low for the middle player to catch it and should travel towards player 3 at the end who should reach out with arms outstretched and fingers spread to receive the ball. Tell the receiver they may move their feet if necessary to retrieve the ball. Tell the children in the middle that however difficult, they should try to catch the ball. Finally, make sure that you regularly tell the children on the outside to change places with the player in the middle so that all the children get a turn at intercepting, bouncing and receiving.

Children could use 'My progess chart 1' on photocopiable page 55 to record how many times they successfully bounce and catch a large ball.

DIFFERENTIATION

If younger children have difficulty in placing the ball, put a small hoop beside the player in the middle so that they can aim at a visual mark when bouncing the ball.

NOW OR LATER

The bounce pass can be replaced by an overarm throw. Tell the children with the ball to stand with their preferred foot and arm back and the ball held close to the shoulder of that side. Tell them to aim at the player at the other end when they throw. Encourage them to throw just above the head of the middle player rather than too high above their head so that the player in the middle has a chance to intercept the ball.

ESCAPE YOUR PARTNER

OBJECTIVES

To enable children to:
■ practise dodging and feinting skills
■ practise overarm throwing
■ experience a mini-team situation.

RESOURCES AND CLASS MANAGEMENT

Children work in groups of four. Each group will need one large ball between them.

WHAT TO DO

Tell the children that they are going to play two against two and use overarm throws to move the ball between one another. Ask each group to split into two pairs and decide who is to start with the ball. Explain that the children must each decide which of the other two players they are going to mark when they have the ball. The two pairs stand facing each other. Player 1 holds the ball and looks towards their partner, player 4. Player 4 stands besides player 3 who is partnering player 2. Tell player 4 who is to receive the ball that, using the upper part of the body, they should quickly bend right then left and right again before sprinting to the left trying to lose their marker, player 3. Then, as they lose their marker, they should raise their left hand high to signal to the player with the ball. It will help children to learn if you can demonstrate this part of the activity. At this point, the player with the ball throws overarm, with their preferred foot and hand back, to the player who is signalling. The marker tries to intercept by moving in front of the receiver. The fourth player remains close to the player with the ball so that when the ball has been thrown, they can mark that player and try to intercept the return throw.

Tell the children to carry on the throwing, marking and dodging. If you think that the ball is remaining too long with one pair of children, tell them to hand it over to the other pair so all children practise all the skills.

DIFFERENTIATION

Younger children or those less able may do this practice in groups of three with one person throwing, one receiving and one marking. Make sure they regularly change over so they can all practise the skills involved.

NOW OR LATER

When children have regularly practised this activity, let them try with no restriction on the types of throws that can be used. Tell them that if the distance is short, they can make a chest pass. If the marker is very good at marking, they should try a bounce pass. Encourage the children to practise these throws in pairs beforehand, possibly in the warm-up or using an activity from the skills section, so they are reminded of the technique.

CROSS-CURRICULAR LINKS
ATHLETICS
Participating in competitions that call for precision, speed, power or stamina.

These games cover all versions of rounders and cricket and should be used in the summer term of each year. Most schools will have access to a field and all the activities are suitable for use on grass unless stated under 'Resources and class management' in the individual activity. However, if the weather is poor or if it is particularly wet underfoot, they can all be adapted for use on a hard surface both inside and outside.

The activities in this section focus on:
■ practising bowling a ball underarm
■ aiming at a target
■ retrieving a loose ball
■ learning batting skills
■ passing a ball to team members in a variety of ways
■ working co-operatively in small groups.

BOWL AND BAT

OBJECTIVES

To enable children to:
■ practise underarm bowling
■ use batting skills
■ aim at a target.

RESOURCES AND CLASS MANAGEMENT

Children work in pairs. Each child will need a round, flat bat of any size and a small tennis or rubber ball between each pair. Copies of photocopiable page 56 are optional for each child.

WHAT TO DO

Tell the children they are going to practise a bowling and batting activity. Ask each pair to decide who is going to start with the bat and who is going to start with the ball. The children should find a space and stand facing each other about four paces apart. The player with the bat holds it in their preferred hand and raises it to shoulder level with the arm bent at the elbow and the foot on the same side behind. The player holding the ball (the bowler), swings their preferred arm back and at the same time puts the leg on that side of the body back so that the body weight is on the back foot. They swing their arm forward and release the ball at shoulder height, aiming for the centre of their partner's bat. The body weight should come forward onto the front foot as they release the ball. Tell the player with the bat to swing the arm holding the bat back as they see the ball coming towards them, and hit it as hard as they can.

After they have done this several times, tell them to change over equipment. Explain that the bowler always retrieves the ball.

Children can use 'My progress chart 2' on photocopiable page 56 to record their achievements in bowling, batting and retrieving the ball.

DIFFERENTIATION

Remind younger children how to throw underarm to each other and encourage them to practise before introducing the bat. Children who find this difficult can use a flat hand to hit the ball before using a bat. Younger or less able children should be given a bat with a large surface area to make it easier to hit the ball.

NOW OR LATER

When the children are more accomplished at this activity, tell the children who are batting to try and hit the ball back to the bowler who should try and catch it with two hands. Explain that in order to be very accurate, the batter should turn sideways but keep watching the ball.

KNOCK THE SKITTLE

RESOURCES AND CLASS MANAGEMENT

Children work individually. Each child will need a large or medium sized-ball and a skittle or a piece of apparatus to use as a target. If equipment is not available for every child, the children can work in groups with one ball and a skittle between each group. Copies of photocopiable page 56 are optional for each child.

WHAT TO DO

Tell the children to place the skittle upright on the ground and move seven paces away from it. Tell them they are going to use a variety of throws, rolls and bounces to knock over the skittle and score points. The children should hold the ball with both hands, close to the ground and on one side of the body. The leg and foot should be placed back on that side of the body. Tell the children to swing their arm back then forward, releasing the ball early so that it rolls along the ground towards the skittle. Explain that if they swing it with some degree of force, it will be more likely to knock over the skittle if it is aimed correctly. When the ball has reached the target, tell them to run and retrieve the ball before trying again.

When they have tried this three or four times, change the way they aim by throwing the ball instead of rolling it. Tell them to hold the ball at their right or left shoulder with the same leg and foot behind and the hands in front of and behind the ball with fingers spread. Tell them to push the ball from the shoulder towards the skittle and try and knock it over. Repeat this several times, then try alternating the throwing and rolling.

Children can use 'My progress chart 2' on photocopiable page 56 to record how many times they hit the target.

DIFFERENTIATION

The activity can be done with either the rolling or the throwing method of aiming if the children are young or find it difficult.

Adjust the distance between the children and the skittle if the children are older or more able.

NOW OR LATER

The children can be told to try a bounce throw and hit the skittle. Tell them to experiment with bouncing the ball close to their own body and then bouncing it nearer the skittle to find out which is the most accurate place to bounce the ball and hit the target. When they are using the bounce pass, remember to tell them to place one foot behind the body so that the body weight starts on the back foot and transfers to the front foot as they push the ball to the ground. If children find it tiring retrieving their own ball each time, they can do the activity in pairs so that one child aims and the other retrieves before changing over.

ROLL, SNATCH AND THROW

RESOURCES AND CLASS MANAGEMENT

Children work in pairs. Each pair will need one small ball, the size of a tennis ball. This activity is best practised on a school field as it slows the ball down to a manageable speed for the children to retrieve it. Copies of photocopiable page 56 for each child are optional.

WHAT TO DO

Ask the children to stand by the side of their partner. Tell the children with the ball

OBJECTIVES

To enable children to:
■ practise aiming skills
■ use different ways of throwing a ball
■ increase the distance between themselves and a target.

OBJECTIVES

To enable children to:
■ work co-operatively with a partner
■ practise rolling and throwing a ball
■ practise retrieving a ball.

CROSS-CURRICULAR
LINKS
ATHLETICS
Participating in challenges
that call for precision, speed
and stamina.

to hold it in one hand and place the foot and leg on that side back, putting the body weight on the back foot. Explain that they are going to swing the arm and hand holding the ball forward and, at the same time, bend the knee of the front leg and lean the body forward so that as they release the ball, it will roll along the ground.

The children without a ball must watch their partner carefully to see when it is released. At that moment, they must run very quickly after the rolling ball to try and get ahead of it before turning, bending forward and scooping up the ball with one hand. Tell them that as they scoop up the ball, they should place the leg and foot on that side of the body back and transfer their body weight to the back foot. As they do this, tell them to straighten the body and bring the ball to shoulder height before throwing it overarm back to their partner and transferring the body weight to the front foot at the same time. Finally, tell the player who initially rolled the ball to stretch out their arms with fingers spread to receive the ball. As the ball arrives in

their hands, they should bring it into the body at chest and waist height. Children can use 'My progress chart 2' on photocopiable page 56 to record the number of times they successfully retrieve the ball.

DIFFERENTIATION
Less able children can practise this with a larger ball so that they can retrieve it with both hands if necessary.

NOW OR LATER
When the children become more confident, you can give them a skittle or other target to aim for when rolling the ball. Their partner should try and reach the ball before it hits the target. The target needs to be placed about ten metres from the children who are rolling the ball.

HOOP BOUNCE

OBJECTIVES
To enable children to:
■ aim at a target
■ practise a bounce pass
■ practise catching and
retrieving a ball.

RESOURCES AND CLASS MANAGEMENT
Children work in pairs. Each pair will need one small hoop and one small rubber or tennis ball. This activity is best practised on a hard surface such as a playground or a hall or, indeed, the field if it is very dry and hard.

WHAT TO DO
Each pair should stand facing one other about ten paces apart with the hoop placed flat on the ground halfway between them. Explain that they are going to aim at the hoop and bounce the ball inside it before it reaches their partner. Tell the children with the ball to hold it in one hand with their fingers spread over the top of the ball and with the leg and foot on that side of their body back and the body weight on the back foot. Make sure they know that as they push the ball and aim to bounce it in the hoop, the body weight should transfer to the front foot. Tell the children receiving the ball that they should stretch out their arms with hands cupped and fingers spread to receive it. As they catch it, they should bring it into the centre of the body. They should then bounce the ball back to their partner.

Tell the children to repeat this activity aiming to keep the bouncing and catching going in a fluent movement phrase.

DIFFERENTIATION

Younger or less able children can work with larger hoops and bigger balls.

Older and more capable children can be encouraged to work with very small hoops, even quoits, if possible.

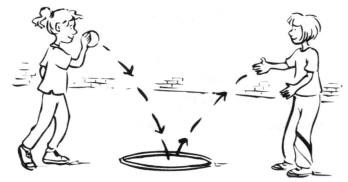

NOW OR LATER

When the children can do this activity with some degree of accuracy, exchange the hoops for a chalk mark on the ground, for example a cross, and ask them to try aiming the ball at the centre point of the cross.

THROW AND RUN

RESOURCES AND CLASS MANAGEMENT

Children work in pairs. Each pair will need one small ball. This activity is best carried out when you have access to a field as the distances involved are fairly big. Copies of photocopiable page 58 for each child are optional.

WHAT TO DO

Tell the children that this is an activity where the ball will be thrown by one player and retrieved by another. Explain that it will help them retrieve a loose ball. Tell the children to stand side by side and face a direction where they have a clear space of half a playing field length ahead of them. You can make this easier by asking the children to stand in a line all facing the same way. The children with the ball should stand with their preferred hand and foot back and hold the ball at shoulder height with their body weight on the back foot. Tell them to push the ball hard from the shoulder and at the same time transfer their body weight from the back foot to the front foot. As they release the ball, tell them to shout the command, *Go!* On hearing this command, their partner must run hard after the ball either trying to catch it before it comes down to the ground or retrieving it from the ground as quickly as possible.

When the ball has been retrieved, tell the children to run with it back to their partner's side and get ready to be the player who throws the ball. Make sure the children are aware that they should throw the ball some distance but at the same time give their partner a reasonable chance of retrieving it quickly. If you see a child throwing the correct distance, ask them to demonstrate to the remainder of the class.

It may be appropriate for children to use 'My fitness record' on photocopiable page 58 to investigate the effect of exercise on their pulse rates during this activity.

DIFFERENTIATION

A larger ball can be used for younger or less able children. If the children find it difficult to judge the throwing distance, use a line if there is one, or use skipping ropes to make your own line and tell the children to throw to the line.

OBJECTIVES

To enable children to:
■ practise overarm throwing
■ practise retrieving a loose ball
■ work co-operatively with another player.

CROSS-CURRICULAR LINKS
SCIENCE
Investigating the effect of rest and exercise on pulse rate.

NOW OR LATER

When the children are familiar with this activity, tell the children to aim to throw the ball higher than head height so that their partner can try and run and catch the ball before it reaches the ground. You will need to tell the children to throw a shorter distance than before if their partner is going to have a realistic chance of catching the ball.

HIT, BOUNCE, HIT

OBJECTIVES

To enable children to:
■ practise bouncing a ball with a bat
■ work co-operatively with a partner
■ perform a sequence of movements.

CROSS-CURRICULAR LINKS

GYMNASTICS

Creating and perform fluent sequences

RESOURCES AND CLASS MANAGEMENT

Children work in pairs. Each pair will need one small ball which will bounce, for example a tennis ball or a rubber ball. They will also need a circular bat each, either made of wood or plastic, or tennis rackets for older children will suffice. This activity is best carried out on a hard surface to aid the bouncing action such as a playground or hall surface, or a playing field if it is dry and hard.

WHAT TO DO

Ask the children to collect a bat each and a ball between the two of them. Explain to them that they are going to take it in turns to bounce the ball to the ground in a controlled manner and try and keep a sequence of movement going. The children should stand by their partner's side. Tell the children holding a ball that using their hand, they must make the first bounce and thereafter they must hit the ball to the ground using their bat.

The important point to emphasize is that they must try each time to hit the ball with the centre of their bat and in a straight line down to the ground. This will give sufficient control to their hit so that their partner is able to do the same thing when the ball rises again. The sequence of movement should be as follows: player 1 pushes the ball to the ground using a hand, player 2 waits for the ball to rise then pushes it to the ground with their bat followed by player 1 pushing it to the ground using their bat. This sequence should be continued for as long as possible.

DIFFERENTIATION

Younger or less able children can begin by using one bat and one ball with player 1 pushing the ball with their hand to the ground and as it rises, player 2 using the bat to push it to the ground. Make sure you tell the children to change over at regular intervals so they both have a go at using a bat and their hand.

NOW OR LATER

When the children have practised this activity and have some degree of competence, tell them to stand one behind the other facing the same direction. The player in front should have the ball and bounce it, using a hand, on the ground in front of their foot. As soon as the ball is dropped, that player moves quickly behind their partner who should be ready with their bat to move forward and push the ball to the ground. They should then move quickly out of the way in order to make room for their partner to have the next go.

The activities in this section focus on:
■ encouraging team work
■ introducing an element of competition
■ giving opportunities to practise bowling and aiming a ball
■ giving opportunities to improve hitting skills
■ preparing to play mini-games.
The photocopiable sheet 'How should I behave?' on page 62 can be used in conjunction with any of these activities.

THREE STAR BATTING

RESOURCES AND CLASS MANAGEMENT
Children work in groups of three. Each group will need a small ball the size of a tennis ball but this can be made from any material. Each child will also need a circular, flat bat made of wood or strong plastic. Copies of photocopiable pages 56 and 61 for each child are optional.

WHAT TO DO
Ask each group of children to collect one bat and one ball between them. Explain that the child hitting the ball should be facing the bowler approximately five or six strides apart. The third member of the group, the fielder, should place themselves diagonally facing the hitter and some distance away. Tell the children holding the bat to raise it to shoulder level on the preferred side of the body and turn the body sideways with the leg and foot back on that side.

The bowler must aim for the middle of the bat and throw underarm towards it. Remind the bowlers to have the same leg and foot back as they swing the arm back to throw the ball. Tell them to transfer the weight of the body onto the front foot as they release the ball. The hitter should watch the ball carefully then, just before the ball arrives, they should swing back the hitting arm and bring it forward to hit the ball as hard as they can. The photocopiable page 61 'Circle the mistakes' may be useful here to remind children how they should stand ready to bat.

The fielder must run quickly to field the ball and scoop it up before throwing to the bowler. If the fielder is close to the bowler, they should throw using an underarm throw but if they are far away they should throw using an overarm pass, always adjusting the feet first so that the leg on the throwing side is back. Warn the fielders that the hitter may miss the ball and they may have to run behind the hitter to field it.

Finally, explain to the children that each hitter has three turns and they score a point every time they hit the ball. Make sure everyone gets a turn at each position by moving them around in a circle at regular intervals. At the completion of the practice, ask each group to add up their hitting scores and compare them with the other groups. This lays the foundation for working as a team to build up scores to compete against other teams.

Children can use 'My progress chart 2' on photocopiable page 56 to record their 'runs'.

DIFFERENTIATION
Younger or less able children can practise this activity by using their hand as a bat. The balls used in this case should be either of sponge material or lightweight plastic.

Older children can begin with large circular bats and progress to smaller bats as they improve.

OBJECTIVES
To enable children to:
■ practise batting and underarm bowling skills
■ practise retrieving a ball
■ work co-operatively.

CROSS-CURRICULAR LINKS
ATHLETICS
Taking part in challenges which call for precision, speed, power or stamina.

Now or later

When the children have practised this activity on a number of occasions, you can introduce a fourth player who stands behind the hitter to field any ball which is not hit by the batsman. Tell them to stand behind the batsman at a distance of approximately three strides.

Touch skittle

Resources and class management

Children work in groups of three. Each group will need one small ball of any composition and one skittle or piece of apparatus that will stand upright. Copies of photocopiable page 56 for each child are optional.

What to do

It is useful at the beginning of this practice to explain to the children that this is an activity which prepares them to play rounders and that, in a rounders game, the catcher would be a batter.

Ask each group of children to collect one ball and one skittle between them. Let the children decide who will be bowler, catcher and fielder in each group. Then tell them to position themselves so that they stand in a triangular shape with the fielder standing by the side of the skittle and the bowler and catcher facing each other. Adjust the distances between the children according to ability and age.

The bowler will hold the ball in their preferred hand and swing the arm back putting their body weight on the back foot on the same side. As the arm is swung forward, the ball should be released at shoulder height with the body weight transferring to the front foot. The catcher reaches forward with outstretched arms and fingers spread to receive the ball, then pulls it into the body at about chest height. After adjusting the feet so that the same leg and arm are back, the catcher will bring the ball up to their preferred shoulder before pushing it strongly towards the fielder. The fielder will receive the ball in the same way as the catcher, then will touch the top of the skittle with the ball before adjusting their feet and throwing overarm to the bowler. Encourage the children to try and get a rhythm going so that the actions of bowl, catch, throw, catch, stump the post and throw, are not interrupted by the ball flying loose. Finally, after a number of attempts, move the children in a circle to another position so that eventually, each child gets a turn in every position.

Children can use 'My progress chart 2' on photocopiable page 56 to record the number of times they bowl and catch the ball and stump the post.

DIFFERENTIATION

Younger or less able children can use larger balls and/or use underarm throwing instead of overarm throwing.

Encourage older children to count the number of times the ball goes around the circle before it is dropped.

NOW OR LATER

When the children are skilled at this practice, position the fielder at a distance from the skittle so that when the ball is caught by the fielder, he or she has to run towards the skittle in order to stump it, then throw it to the bowler as before.

BASE TOUCH

RESOURCES AND CLASS MANAGEMENT

Children work in groups of three. Each group will need a tennis ball or a small rubber ball, a circular wooden or strong plastic bat and a skittle or an upright post. Copies of photocopiable page 56 for each child are optional.

WHAT TO DO

Explain to the children that this activity will help them when they play rounders and cricket. Ask each group to decide who will be bowler, batter and backstop, then collect one skittle, one ball and one bat. Tell the children to position themselves so that the bowler stands beside the skittle, the hitter stands facing the bowler approximately six or seven paces away and the backstop stands approximately two paces behind the hitter, facing their back. Before the children begin, remind them that whatever throw they use, the leg and foot on the same side as the preferred arm should be back.

When the children are in position, explain that the bowler will throw underarm and aim to get the ball in the hands of the backstop whilst the batter will try to have the bat ready to hit the ball. If the ball is hit, the batter gains a point and the backstop runs to field the ball. If the ball is not hit, the backstop should be ready, hands cupped at chest or stomach level, to anticipate catching the ball. After the batter has had several turns, ask the children to change position. Make sure that the children have a turn at all the positions in the activity before asking them how many points they have gained. You can either let them compete and score points on an individual basis or you can let them add together the group's score to compete against the other groups in the class.

Children can use 'My progress chart 2' on photocopiable page 56 to record successful hits.

OBJECTIVES

To enable children to:
■ practise batting and bowling skills
■ practise retrieving a loose ball
■ experience a competitive activity.

CROSS-CURRICULAR LINKS
ATHLETICS
Using running and throwing skills in combination.

DIFFERENTIATION

Younger or less able children can use their hand to hit the ball and they can also use larger balls.

Older or more able children can use rounders balls instead of balls made of rubber but if they do, the bats need to be wooden.

NOW OR LATER

When the children are very familiar with this activity, tell them that when the hitter strikes the ball they must run quickly towards the skittle and touch it before returning to their position. One point is scored for each successful run but if the ball is not struck, the hitter remains still.

BALL SNATCH

OBJECTIVES

To enable children to:
- retrieve a moving ball
- practise accurate passing
- work co-operatively.

RESOURCES AND CLASS MANAGEMENT

Children work in groups of three. Each group will need a tennis ball or a small rubber ball. Copies of photocopiable page 56 for each child are optional.

WHAT TO DO

Tell each group of children to collect one ball between them and number themselves 1, 2 and 3. Explain that they should make the shape of a triangle with number 1 holding the ball and facing number 2, and number 3 making the third point of the triangle to the left or right. The distance between numbers 1 and 2 needs to be at least 25 metres. Explain to the children that numbers 1 and 2 will roll the ball backwards and forwards to each other. Number 3 will run quickly across to try and retrieve it from the ground before it reaches the receiving player each time.

Remind the children who are rolling the ball that the arm and leg on their preferred side should be back and, as they swing the arm forward to release the ball, the weight should be transferred onto the front foot with the upper body bent well forward so that the ball is released along the ground. Number 3 should begin their run in as the ball is released. They should stretch out their arms and hands in preparation before they reach the ball. As they scoop up the ball they should continue running a short distance so that they do not stop suddenly with the possibility of hurting themselves. If number 3 successfully fields the ball, they swap places with the player who rolled the ball. If the ball is not fielded successfully, however, then number 3 returns to their place to try again. Make sure that during the course of the activity every player gets a turn at rolling and retrieving the ball.

Children can use 'My progress chart 2' on photocopiable page 56 to record how many times they retrieve the ball.

DIFFERENTIATION

Younger children may find this practice easier if they begin by using a large ball then progress to a medium-sized ball before finally using a small ball. Distances between players 1 and 2 can be decreased to six or seven strides.

NOW OR LATER

Children can progress from this practice to passing the ball to another player after it has been retrieved from the ground. Tell player 3 to retrieve the ball as before, then adjust their feet so that they are ready to throw under or overarm to player 1 or 2, with preferred arm and leg back and weight on the back foot. You can introduce a fourth player at this stage so that if the ball is fielded by player 3, they can throw it to player 4 who throws it back to player 1 or 2. Children can score points if they successfully retrieve the ball.

COUNTING SHUTTLE

RESOURCES AND CLASS MANAGEMENT

Children work in groups of four. Each group will need one tennis ball or other small ball.

WHAT TO DO

Ask the children to collect one small ball between them, then find a space and form a circle by holding hands with arms outstretched, then releasing hands. This circle can then be adjusted by taking steps backwards to make it bigger. The children should number themselves, 1 to 4. One player in each group holds the ball ready to begin. The player with the ball throws it up in the air to a height of approximately one metre above their head, then takes one step backwards and calls out a number between 1 and 4, disregarding their own number. As the number is called out, the correct player runs quickly towards the ball until they are underneath it. They stretch up their arms and hands with fingers outstretched to catch the ball and pull it into the body at about chest height. The child who has caught the ball returns to their place in the circle and repeats the sequence making sure they do not call out their own number. If the ball is dropped or not caught first time, the child who threw the ball must retrieve it then take it back to their place in the circle. Point out to the children that they can repeat a number on two consecutive occasions in order to keep the other players alert and ready to move.

DIFFERENTIATION

Younger or less able children can be told to bounce the ball in front of them before calling out a number and taking a step backwards. Alternatively, a large ball can be used by the groups.

OBJECTIVES

To enable children to:
■ practise accuracy in throwing up a ball
■ react quickly in a team situation
■ practise catching and/or retrieving a ball.

37

Older or more able children can take one or two long strides backwards to make the circle bigger so that the players have to move very quickly in order to catch the ball.

NOW OR LATER
When the children have practised this activity and have some degree of competence, tell the children who are running to catch the ball that when they have caught it, they are going to replace the child who threw it up. That child must throw the ball up, call out a number, step backwards and then run to replace the player who is moving to catch the ball.

THREE VERSUS THREE

OBJECTIVES
To enable children to:
■ experience a small team game
■ practise bowling and batting a ball
■ practise fielding and retrieving a ball.

CROSS-CURRICULAR LINKS
SCIENCE
Investigating the effect of exercise and rest on pulse rate.

RESOURCES AND CLASS MANAGEMENT
Children work in groups of six. Each group will need a rounders ball and a rounders bat. However, this activity can be done equally well using a cricket bat and ball. Copies of photocopiable pages 56 and 58 for each child are optional.

WHAT TO DO
Explain to the children that they are going to play mini-rounders with three against three. One team of three children will bat and one team will field with one bowler, one backstop and one fielder. Each batting team will have three chances to hit the ball and score a point for their team. It is best if they take turns to have one hit each before having their second and third hits so that each child stays involved in the game.

The bowler in the fielding team should pace five strides away from the batting team, then turn to face the first batter and bowl underarm to try and allow the backstop who is standing behind the batter, to catch the ball. The batter should raise the bat to shoulder height at either their right or left side, and try to hit the ball. If the ball is successfully hit, the fielder runs and retrieves it then adjusts their feet to throw overarm back to the bowler. Remind the fielders that as they throw overarm, right-handers should have their right foot back and left-handers, their left foot back. If the ball is not hit then it becomes the backstop's responsibility to field it and throw overarm back to the bowler. When the batting team have each had three tries, the teams change over.

Children can use 'My progress chart 2' on photocopiable page 56 to record how many times they hit the ball and it may be appropriate for children to use 'My fitness record' on page 58 to investigate the effect of exercise on their pulse rates.

DIFFERENTIATION
Younger children can use round wooden bats and small plastic, rubber or tennis balls for this activity. If the children find this difficult, they can use their hand as a bat and a soft sponge ball. This enables them to experience a team situation without using the hard equipment.

Older or more able children can move around the positions on the field when they are not batting. They can each have a turn at being bowler, backstop and fielder to practise their skills at all the positions.

NOW OR LATER
You can introduce a skittle as a base post for the children to run to whether they are playing mini-rounders or mini-cricket. When the ball has been hit, the player who hit it should be told to run quickly to the post and touch it with their bat. If they hit a long way, they can run back to score a second run. When the ball is in the hands of the bowler, the hitter must stop running and return to their place.

NET AND WALL GAMES
SKILLS FOR ONE OR TWO PLAYERS

The activities in this section use skills that are applicable to short tennis, tennis and wall games. Some of the activities can be adapted if wall space is limited or unavailable in the school (see under 'Resources and class management' in individual activities). Generally, these activities will be used in the summer term when tennis and wall games are played. Distances mentioned in the activities are suggestions only and can be adapted to suit the age and ability of the class.

Many of these activities are more suited to practice on a hard surface such as a playground or school hall. However, they can be used on a playing field if the conditions are dry and the ground is hard.

The activities in this section focus on:
- using techniques to improve aiming skills
- practising hitting skills
- working co-operatively
- increasing ball skills
- keeping a ball in motion
- using techniques to alter the speed of a ball.

BACK AND FRONT BOUNCING

RESOURCES AND CLASS MANAGEMENT
Children work independently. Each child will need a tennis racket and a small ball. Copies of photocopiable pages 57 and 61 for each child are optional.

WHAT TO DO
Tell the children to hold their racket in one hand and the ball in the other. Explain that they are going to hold the racket with the flat side uppermost, like a frying pan, throw the ball up in the air and gently tap it with the racket in order to keep it up in the air. You may find it useful to use the photocopiable sheet 'Circle the mistakes' on page 61 to remind children about holding rackets in a position of readiness to hit a ball. Emphasize that they should not try and hit the ball too high and they may have to move their feet in order to repeat the hit. Tell them to tap the ball three times into the air and then turn their wrist over so that the next three taps are done with the racket in a backhand position. They should repeat this sequence until the ball drops or you tell them to stop.

Children can use 'My progress chart 3' on photocopiable page 57 to record the number of times they hit the ball with the racket.

DIFFERENTIATION
Less able children can practise this activity in pairs, with one player hitting the ball upward and their partner catching the ball with cupped hands before throwing it up to be hit by the player with the racket.

Older children can be set targets, for example trying to keep the sequence going for three sets of hits before dropping the ball.

NOW OR LATER
A variation on this activity is to tap the ball in the air, then let it bounce once on the ground before placing the racket underneath the ball and hitting it in the air again. Remind the children to try and aim the ball in a straight line upward so that they do not have to move their feet excessively.

OBJECTIVES
To enable children to:
- improve bat and ball control
- maintain a ball in motion
- increase concentration spans.

CROSS-CURRICULAR LINKS
ATHLETICS
Taking part in challenges that call for precision.

AIM THE HIT

OBJECTIVES

To enable children to:
- practise aiming skills
- improve racket skills
- work co-operatively.

RESOURCES AND CLASS MANAGEMENT

Children work in pairs. Each pair will need a tennis racket and a small tennis-sized ball.

WHAT TO DO

Tell the children to collect one racket and one small ball between each pair. One player holds the ball and the other player holds the racket and they stand facing each other approximately ten strides apart. Explain that the player with the ball will bounce the ball to the player with the racket who will hit the ball and try and aim to get the ball back into the hands of the first player. Remind the children that when bouncing or hitting the ball, right-handed players should have their right foot back and left-handed players should have their left foot back. As the ball is released or hit, their body weight should transfer from the back foot to the front foot. Encourage the players with the racket to stand sideways to hit the ball. Emphasize the need for accurate bouncing and hitting each time and make sure the children regularly change over so that they practise both bouncing and hitting.

DIFFERENTIATION

Younger or less able children can begin by using their hand as a bat and a plastic ball to bounce.

Older children can be encouraged to increase the distance between themselves and their partner but only as far as they can continue to maintain an accurate hit into or near the hands of the receiver.

NOW OR LATER

When the children have improved accuracy skills, tell the player with the racket to hit the ball higher but shorter in distance so that the other child has to run forward and, with hands cupped, try and catch the ball. This prepares children to move their feet to reach a ball when they play short tennis as a game.

TO AND FRO

OBJECTIVES

To enable children to:
- become accustomed to practising with a net
- improve accuracy skills
- practise hitting techniques.

RESOURCES AND CLASS MANAGEMENT

Children work in pairs. Each pair will need access to a tennis net or similar and the use of one tennis racket and a small ball.

WHAT TO DO

Ask the children to collect one racket and one ball between them, then face each other on opposite sides of the net. Explain that the player with the ball will throw it underarm over the net and the player with the racket will let it bounce on the ground once before hitting it back to their partner, aiming to get the ball into or near their partner's cupped hands. Remind the players using the racket to stand sideways to hit the ball and explain that they will need to lift the ball slightly as they hit it so that it goes over the net. Remind both players that they should position their feet so that the same hand and foot are back each time when throwing or hitting.

Make sure that the children regularly change over equipment so that both players practise hitting and throwing.

DIFFERENTIATION

Children who are inexperienced at throwing or hitting over a net can begin this activity by throwing the ball to each other and letting it bounce before catching it.

NOW OR LATER

When the children have had some success with this activity, you can let each child have a racket to hit the ball over the net to one another. Tell them that when receiving the ball, they should always let it bounce. To begin the action, the first child should bounce the ball in front of their leading foot then hit it as it rises from the ground.

HIGH AND LOW THROWING

RESOURCES AND CLASS MANAGEMENT

Children work in pairs. Each pair will need a tennis ball or similar small ball and access to a net or suitable obstacle. If there are no nets available, two benches from the school hall or gym can be stacked with the two wide surfaces together to create a workable obstacle. At a later stage, the children will need plastic or lightweight balls instead of tennis balls. Copies of photocopiable page 57 for each child are optional.

WHAT TO DO

Ask the children to collect one small ball between each pair and stand facing their partner on opposite sides of the obstacle. Explain that they are going to throw the ball underarm to each other, varying the height of the ball so that player I throws

OBJECTIVES

To enable children to:
■ practise throwing and hitting over an obstacle
■ practise accuracy skills
■ increase speed of footwork.

CROSS-CURRICULAR LINKS

GYMNASTICS
Creating and performing fluent sequences.

the ball to clear the obstacle with a small margin and player 2 throws the ball to clear the obstacle by a high margin. Remind the children that right-handers should begin with their right foot back and left-handers should begin with their left foot back. Their body weight should be transferred to the front foot as the ball is released from the hand. Emphasize that if the ball is released early, in other words, below shoulder height, it will travel lower than if it is released above shoulder height when it will travel higher.

Tell the children that as they reach forward to catch the ball with cupped hands, they should bring the ball into the centre of the body before releasing one hand and preparing to throw once more. The fluidity of the movement is important as well as the accuracy of throwing at the required height. Finally, make sure you tell the children to change regularly so that they each have a chance to throw low and high.

DIFFERENTIATION

Less able children can concentrate on throwing and catching across the obstacle without the height restriction.

Older and more able children can set themselves target numbers to see how many times they can throw and catch high and low without dropping the ball. Children can use 'My progress chart 3' on photocopiable page 57 to record their throws and catches.

NOW OR LATER

A progression of this practice is for player 1 to throw the ball as before and player 2 to use their hand with flat palm as a bat to hit the ball back to player 1 who retrieves it and repeats the throw. It is preferable to use plastic or other lightweight balls for this. Remind the children who are using their hand as a bat that as they hit the ball, they should stand sideways with the same arm and leg back. The arm and hand should be held at shoulder level.

SIDE BY SIDE BATTING

OBJECTIVES

To enable children to:
■ work co-operatively with a partner
■ improve ball control
■ practise hitting skills.

RESOURCES AND CLASS MANAGEMENT

Children work in pairs. Each pair will need two tennis rackets and a tennis ball. Copies of photocopiable pages 57 and 61 for each child are optional.

WHAT TO DO

Ask the children to collect a tennis racket each and a ball between each pair. Tell them to stand by the side of their partner. Explain that they are going to hit the ball straight upward alternately and try and keep the ball in the air. Player 1 throws up the ball for player 2 to hit, then player 1 hits it with the racket for player 2 to hit and so on. This is repeated for as long as the children manage without letting the ball drop to the ground. The racket should be held with flat side uppermost, like a frying pan, with the arm slightly bent in front of the body at chest level. You may find it useful to use the photocopiable sheet 'Circle the mistakes' on photocopiable page 61 to remind children about holding rackets in the correct position. Emphasize that the ball should only be hit hard enough to rise just above the head so that it can be more easily controlled. Tell the children that if the ball is not accurately placed by one of the players, they should be prepared to move quickly to see if they can get the racket under the ball and hit it upward before it drops to the ground.

Children can use 'My progress chart 3' on photocopiable page 57 to record how many times they hit the ball to keep it in the air.

DIFFERENTIATION

Younger or less able children can be allowed to hold the racket with both hands but you will need to continue the emphasis on tapping the ball lightly and as straight upward as possible.

Older children should be encouraged to move their feet quickly in order to keep the ball in the air if it is hit away from them.

NOW OR LATER

When the children have mastered this practice, you can increase the number of children who hit the ball up in turn. Start by having three children in a circle and increase to four when appropriate. Emphasize control of the bat and ball at all times and encourage the children to make it easy for their group to remain still when hitting upward.

HIT AND CATCH

RESOURCES AND CLASS MANAGEMENT

Children work independently. They will each need a tennis racket and small ball. Copies of photocopiable page 57 for each child are optional.

OBJECTIVES

To enable children to:
■ improve racket skills
■ practise ball control
■ practise accurate hitting.

WHAT TO DO

Ask the children to collect a racket and a ball each and stand in a space. Explain that they are going to hit the ball upward with the racket, then allow the ball to bounce on the ground before catching it with the other hand. To initiate the action, the children should throw the ball into the air at a height just above their heads, then let it bounce before placing the racket flat side uppermost, like a frying pan, to gently hit it straight upward before repeating the action. As most children will hold the racket in their preferred hand, it is likely that they will be catching the ball in their non-preferred hand. You may wish to explain that this is a good exercise to prepare for serving in tennis.

Children can use 'My progress chart 3' on photocopiable page 57 to record how many times they hit the ball and catch it.

DIFFERENTIATION

Younger children may find it easier to hold the racket halfway down the handle. This will enable them to exercise more control over it.

Older children should be encouraged to move quickly towards the ball if it veers outside their personal space.

NOW OR LATER

This activity can be used to practise a backhand stroke. Tell the children to turn the racket over by rotating their wrist, then hit the ball upward with the other side of the racket. This activity is also suitable for encouraging children to change over hands and use their non-preferred hand for hitting and their preferred hand for catching.

43

The activities in this section focus on:
- improving ball control
- keeping a ball in play
- using backhand and forehand strokes with a racket
- practising hitting a ball with accuracy
- practising retrieving a ball in a variety of ways
- working co-operatively.

The photocopiable sheet 'How should I behave?' on page 60 can be used in conjunction with any of these activities.

TRIO CATCHING

OBJECTIVES

To enable children to:
- learn to catch a ball on the rebound
- practise accurate throwing
- work co-operatively.

RESOURCES AND CLASS MANAGEMENT

Children work in groups of three. Each group will need a tennis ball or a small rubber ball that will bounce well. They will also require access to a high wall with a hard surface in front of it. Copies of photocopiable page 57 for each child are optional.

WHAT TO DO

Ask the children to collect one ball between each group of three and stand one behind the other in a line, facing the wall and approximately seven paces away from it. The player in front holds the ball. Explain that the player with the ball is going to

throw it at the wall then run behind the line of children. The next player will let the ball rebound and bounce before catching it, then throwing it at the wall before running to the back of the line. The third player repeats these actions and play continues in this way.

If the children find the ball is rebounding too quickly, tell them to throw it higher up the wall which will slow down its speed. You may also have to remind them to adjust their distance from the wall if necessary. Remind the children that when throwing, right-handers should swing their right arm and leg back and left-handers should swing their left arm and leg back. Make sure the children are aware that keeping their eye on the ball is of paramount importance.

Children can use 'My progress chart 3' on photocopiable page 57 to record how many times they catch the ball from the rebound.

DIFFERENTIATION

Less able children can begin this activity working on their own to build up their confidence before working in a group.

More able children can lower the height at which they throw the ball and speed up the rebound and bounce so that the activity is practised at a faster pace.

NOW OR LATER

When the children are regularly catching the ball with confidence, tell them to throw it at the wall and step to the back of the line as before but as the next player steps in, tell them to catch the ball off the rebound without waiting for it to bounce. It is wise to suggest that at the beginning, the children throw the ball fairly high up the wall so that the rebound is slower and they have time to catch it more comfortably.

BATTING CHALLENGE

RESOURCES AND CLASS MANAGEMENT

Children work in groups of four. Each group will need three tennis rackets or circular plastic bats and three tennis balls or other small balls. They will also need to play over a tennis net or a rope which can be raised and maintained at approximately waist level. Copies of photocopiable page 57 for each child are optional.

WHAT TO DO

Tell each group of children to collect three balls and three tennis rackets. Ask them to number themselves players 1, 2, 3 and 4. Player 1 holds the balls and stands on one side of the net, several paces from it and facing players 2, 3 and 4 who are on the other side of the net. They each hold a racket and stand one behind the other, facing the net but with a large area in front of them. Explain that player 1 is going to throw one ball underarm over the net. Player 2 must let it bounce before moving forward, stopping and hitting it with a forehand stroke over the net. Player 2 then runs to the side then to the back of the queue and player 1 throws a ball for player 3 to hit and then another ball for player 4 to hit. Each time the players must let the ball bounce before hitting it.

Before starting this activity, tell the children that before they hit the ball, they must swing back their preferred arm and place the leg and foot on the same side back. They should also turn the body sideways making sure that they have stopped the running movement. As the ball is hit, tell them to continue swinging the racket forward until it reaches the mid-line of their body. Remind the children throwing the ball to place their preferred hand and arm back as well as the leg and foot on the same side of the body.

OBJECTIVES

To enable children to:
■ practise hitting a forehand stroke
■ practise controlled footwork
■ improve ball skills.

When the balls have been hit by all three players, tell them to run and pick them up and begin the activity again but with a different player throwing the balls.

Children can use 'My progress chart 3' on photocopiable page 57 to record how many times they hit the ball over the net.

DIFFERENTIATION

Younger or less able children may start this activity in pairs. Tell the player throwing the ball to pick it up before changing over to try and hit the ball.

Older and more able children can be encouraged to hit the ball and try and place it in a certain spot on the ground, for example to the right or left of the player throwing the ball.

NOW OR LATER

When the children are regularly hitting the ball, tell the players with the racket that they are going to try and hit the ball without letting it bounce first. This may mean that the player throwing the ball needs to aim at a higher spot as the ball goes over the net. The player with the racket should then be encouraged to hit the ball, while it is high, downward towards the ground.

WALL TENNIS

RESOURCES AND CLASS MANAGEMENT

Children work in groups of three. Each group will need one tennis ball and three tennis rackets. They will need access to a high wall with a hard surface in front of it. Copies of photocopiable page 57 for each child are optional.

WHAT TO DO

Ask the children to collect one tennis racket each and one ball between the group of three. Tell them to number themselves 1, 2 and 3. Explain that player 1 will not use their racket until later but will need to have the ball. Player 1 will stand seven or eight long paces from the wall and remain facing it. Players 2 and 3 will stand to the left of and behind player 1.

Tell player 1 that they will throw the ball underarm to hit the wall and then move quickly to their right. Player 2 will run forward and slightly right to position themselves sideways on to the ball, let it bounce on the ground and hit it back to the wall at an angle higher than their head. Player 2 then runs to their right and player 3 runs quickly forward and slightly right to repeat the above. If the ball is not hit or rebounds at an awkward angle, player 1 will be responsible for retrieving it.

Remind all the players that when throwing or hitting, right-handers will have their right foot back and left-handers will have their left foot back. Encourage the children to follow through with the racket when they have hit the ball. Point out to them that although they are running to position themselves correctly, they must stop when actually hitting the ball.

Children can use 'My progress chart 3' on photocopiable page 57 to record how many times they hit the ball with the racket.

DIFFERENTIATION
If any children are left-handed hitters, they can stand behind and to the right of player 1. When they have hit the ball they move away to their right in order to leave space for the next player to hit the ball.

NOW OR LATER
This activity can be practised with two children instead of three. Player 1 begins by throwing the ball at the wall and moving away and thereafter the players take it in turns to hit the ball before moving out of the way to enable their partner to hit it. Emphasize the importance of the run, stop, hit sequence and make the children aware that if they hit the ball at an angle, it is more likely to go out of play. If wall space is limited, this activity can be practised alongside the 'Batting challenge' activity (see page 45).

CATCH ME

RESOURCES AND CLASS MANAGEMENT
Children work in groups of five. Each group will need a tennis ball or other small ball. You will need a stopwatch with a second hand. Copies of photocopiable page 57 for each child are optional.

WHAT TO DO
Ask the children to collect one ball between each group and arrange themselves in a circle. Explain that they are going to throw the ball underarm at random to any one player in the circle who will immediately throw it to another player who will again throw it to another player. This should be continued with the ball moving as quickly as possible. The ball should sometimes be thrown across the circle and sometimes to the players on either side.

Make sure that the children are aware that they must at all times control the way they throw the ball so that the receiver has the maximum chance of catching it and passing it on. Remind left-handers to swing their left arm and leg back and right-handers to swing their right arm and leg back. If throwing to the players at the side, the player with the ball may have to adjust their feet to position the body correctly before throwing. Players who are waiting to receive the ball should be reminded to watch the ball at all times and stand in a position of readiness to catch it quickly, in other words, feet slightly apart and arms and hands at chest level with hands cupped together.

DIFFERENTIATION
Younger children can begin this practice in pairs and be encouraged to throw as quickly as possible without losing control of the ball. When they begin in a circle, ask

OBJECTIVES
To enable children to:
■ practise ball skills at speed
■ improve hand-eye co-ordination
■ work co-operatively.

them to hold hands with outstretched arms, release arms then take one step backward so that the circle is not too big and they are not throwing long distances.

NOW OR LATER

As soon as the children can keep the ball moving without dropping it, tell them you are going to time them over two or three minutes while they count the number of throws they can do in that time without dropping the ball. Each group can use 'My progress chart 3' on page 57 to record their results and, over a period of time, they can set themselves targets to increase their performance.

1, 2, 3, THROW

OBJECTIVES

To enable children to:
■ practise bouncing a ball with one hand
■ practise accurate throwing
■ improve ball control.

RESOURCES AND CLASS MANAGEMENT

Children work in groups of three. Each group will need a tennis ball or other small ball. Unless the playing field is very dry and hard, this activity is best done on the playground.

WHAT TO DO

Ask the children to collect one ball between each group of three and stand in the shape of a triangle with approximately four paces between each player. Explain that the player with the ball is going to bounce the ball three times on the ground, each time catching the ball with only one hand. Then, immediately after they have caught the ball for the third time, they will throw the ball to one of the other players who will repeat the bouncing before throwing it on to the third player who also repeats the bouncing and throwing. Encourage the children to build up a rhythm when bouncing the ball, using the same force to bounce it each time and trying to aim for the same spot on the ground each time, preferably in front of the right or left foot. Tell them to hold the catching hand in a cup shape out in front of the body so that the ball is caught immediately it rises high enough from the bounce.

When a player is passing the ball to another player, an overarm or underarm throw may be used. Either way, players should be reminded to have their preferred foot back. Finally, when they are consistently catching the ball, encourage the children to slowly build up speed in this activity.

DIFFERENTIATION

Younger children can begin by bouncing and catching the ball once before throwing to the next player.

NOW OR LATER

When the children are familiar with this activity, tell them to use their non-preferred hand for bouncing and catching the ball and for throwing it to the next player. This is an important skill which they will need at a later stage when serving in tennis. If the children find it difficult, persevere in short sessions with this practice until they are more comfortable with it.

BACKHAND BOUNCE

OBJECTIVES

To enable children to:
■ improve the backhand stroke
■ practise accurate returns
■ practise good positioning before hitting a ball.

RESOURCES AND CLASS MANAGEMENT

Children work in groups of three. Each group will need three tennis or plastic rackets and one tennis ball. They will need access to a high wall with a hard surface in front of it but this activity can be adapted for use with a net. Copies of photocopiable page 57 for each group are optional (for 'Now or later' activity).

WHAT TO DO

Ask the children to collect a racket each and one tennis ball between each group of three. Tell them to stand in a line, one behind the other, with the wall on their right-hand side and approximately ten paces from the wall. The front player of each group will hold the ball to begin.

Explain that the front player will bounce the ball, then use a backhand stroke to hit it high up the wall, then run forward to leave a clear space for the next player to run, stop and return the ball to the wall after it has bounced on the ground, again using a backhand hit. The second player then moves forward out of the way so that the third player can run in and repeat the activity. When all three players have hit the ball, player 1 retrieves it and the group moves back to their original place with the wall on their right-hand side. Left-handers stand with the wall on their left-hand side.

Tell the children that as they hit the ball with the back of their racket, they should turn the body so that most of their back is facing the wall. The arm should be swung back as far as possible then, when the ball has been hit, the arm should follow the ball through. Right-handers will have the right foot as the leading foot and left-handers, the left foot as the lead.

DIFFERENTIATION

All children can begin this activity independently and should be encouraged to concentrate on moving their feet to position their body sideways on to the wall with their right or left shoulder facing the wall as they hit the ball. Build up to working in pairs, then in threes, when children are moving their feet and positioning their bodies well.

If the children are doing this activity using a net, tell one of the players to throw the ball over the net to the left-hand side of right-handers or the right-hand side of left-handers who then run as before, stop and hit the ball with a backhand stroke across the net. Emphasize throughout this activity that the sequence is run, stop, hit.

NOW OR LATER

A competitive element can be introduced into this activity. When the children are regularly hitting the ball, tell them to count a point every time they hit a successful backhand stroke and add up the group score before asking each group how many points they have scored. Each group can use 'My progress chart 3' on page 57 to record their results.

This section lays the foundations for playing full versions of PE games by applying the basic principles and skills learned in previous sections of this book.
The activities in this section focus on:
■ working co-operatively in groups
■ using a variety of equipment
■ encouraging leadership skills
■ using simple rules within a game
■ practising hitting a target
■ encouraging competition.

MINI-GAMES

The National Curriculum defines a mini-game as 'a small-sided, modified competitive net, striking/fielding or invasion game'. Team and competitive games such as football, hockey, netball, cricket, rounders and tennis can all be played using smaller numbers of players on each team and fewer rules.

To be successful at team games, children must have a bank of skills to call upon including being able to work independently or in pairs or small groups. These skills have been covered in the activities in sections 2, 3 and 4 of this book.

When children have begun to put these skills into practice with some success, they will enjoy playing a modified version of a larger game. The success of the game will depend, to some extent, on the ability of the children and the degree of skill teaching that they have received. However, most children of Year 4 age and above will be capable of sustaining and enjoying small team-game situations. Younger children will still benefit from small competitive situations and games that encourage them to work together and against each other. However, younger children should play games that require a lower degree of bat, ball and throwing skills than required for the games played by older children.

Some of the activities in Sections 2, 3, and 4 in this book can be readily adapted to create mini-games for children in Year 3, for example 'Escape your partner' (Section 2, page 26) and 'Base touch' (Section 3, page 35).

ORGANIZATION OF MINI-GAMES

Organizing mini-games within the PE Curriculum will depend on several factors. You may only have one slot available each week for your class to do games or you may have two. You may have one hour or more each week available for the teaching of games or you may have only 30 minutes per week. You may have a choice or venues such as playground, field or hall or you may be restricted to one venue only. All these factors will need to be considered when deciding when and how to introduce mini-games.

When children are playing mini-games it is tempting for the teacher to make lots of teaching points during the course of the games or spend a lot of the time talking and enforcing rules. One way of increasing the children's skill during the games session is to have a theme for the half term and base the skills and your teaching within the mini-games on that theme. These themes might include: using the space, defending, attacking, ball control, or accuracy in aiming, hitting or throwing.

When organizing teams for the lesson you can have any number of children on each team but two, three or four children on each team will give players a good chance of playing an active role in the mini-game while experiencing a games situation. It is unlikely that many schools will have enough posts and nets for each

50

small team to use during their game but any small post or skittle, chalk marks or hoops can be used to enable players to score goals. Rules should be kept to a minimum and all players should be clear from the start what those rules are. A child from each team can be nominated as a playing referee or umpire, which will free you to circulate and teach every team at some point during the lesson.

PLAYING A MINI-GAME

RESOURCES AND CLASS MANAGEMENT

Children work in groups of three (although the game will also work with small team groups of any number between two and four). Each group will need one large ball, skittles, cones or chalk to act as a target or goal and a set of coloured bands to wear in order to differentiate the teams. You will need a whistle. This activity has been designed as a throwing activity but can equally be used as a kicking or hitting team game, for example a football or hockey mini-game instead of a netball mini-game.

WHAT TO DO

Begin the lesson by choosing two or three warm-up activities so that all the class are well prepared for the skills or mini-game section. Tell the children to get into groups of three, collect a coloured band to wear and go and stand by another group of three children who are wearing a different coloured band. These groups will constitute a three-a-side game. If your class is younger or less able you can put the children into groups of your choice.

Tell the groups of children which area of the playing field or playground they will be allowed to use for their game. Explain to the class that they are going to play a mini-game of netball and must work with their team to try and get the ball to one end of the area and score a goal. To enable the ball to travel around the area, it must be thrown or bounced to another player. You may make the decision as to how the goal will be scored or if you know your class well, you may leave the decision to them but the choices should be:
■ hitting a skittle
■ throwing the ball between two cones or skittles
■ throwing the ball over a chalk line
■ or, if available, shooting the ball into a netball net.
Make sure the teams know which end of the area they will be shooting at and that they are familiar with these rules:
■ that to intercept the ball they must not physically touch another player
■ that any player with the ball must not take more than one step before throwing to another player
■ that if the ball goes out of play, a member of the opposite team should take a free pass at the place it crossed the line.

When the children are clear on the rules, tell them to collect one ball between each three-a-side game and some goalposts or chalk to make a goal at each end of the playing area. When the teams have set up their goals and are in position you may blow a whistle to begin the game. As you will not be in a position to umpire or referee each game it is worthwhile choosing one player from each game who will play and umpire. Older children will find they can do this well with practice and younger children feel it is fairer if they have an umpire on the spot.

NOW OR LATER

■ When you are happy that the children have started their games you may go to each team in turn for a short period of time. During this time you may use your voice to praise a good piece of play but it is a good idea to have decided upon one teaching point which you wish to emphasize during the course of the lesson. A possible teaching point is to make sure the children are throwing correctly (same leg

OBJECTIVES
To enable children to:
■ experience a competitive activity
■ work co-operatively with a small group of children
■ use skills learnt within the context of an activity.

CROSS-CURRICULAR LINKS
PSHE
Working co-operatively and teamwork.

and arm back when throwing) or you could concentrate on encouraging children to use all the space they have available rather than bunching up in a small area. As well as words of praise and encouragement try and stick with the teaching point on which you will base your coaching.

■ At the end of the games lesson tell the children to collect up their equipment and come up to stand in front of you. Ask each team their score and praise and encourage each group. Before ending the lesson choose a cooling-down activity which prepare the children for entry into school.

CREATIVE GAMES

Creative games, or games that the children themselves have made up, are a useful addition to the PE curriculum. They teach the children to work closely together and give them a better understanding of rule-making. Creative games can be introduced at any stage of the games curriculum and you can use them on a regular basis or as a block of lessons before moving on to other activities.

ORGANIZATION OF CREATIVE GAMES

It is usually too time-consuming for a group of children to make up a game with rules and equipment without any guidance and input from you, the teacher. In order that the players have a reasonable length of time to play their game (at least ten minutes), start them off by telling them how big the group should be, the equipment that will be made available to the group and the area they may use to play. Prepare a set of cards beforehand (see example shown below and blank cards on photocopiable page 63) for each group of players. The cards can be reused and will enable you to vary the senarios for the children and ensure that the groups are spread out over the playing area.

Using the pre-prepared cards, the children can organize their own teams and can decide how they are going to use their equipment, how a goal will be scored and what the rules of the game will be. The children might find it helpful to fill in the photocopiable sheet 'Creating a game' on page 62.

When children are confidently making up and playing games you can extend the work by asking one group to teach their game to one of the other groups of children. Some useful discussion work can also take place inside the classroom when talking about the meaning and reason for rule-making.

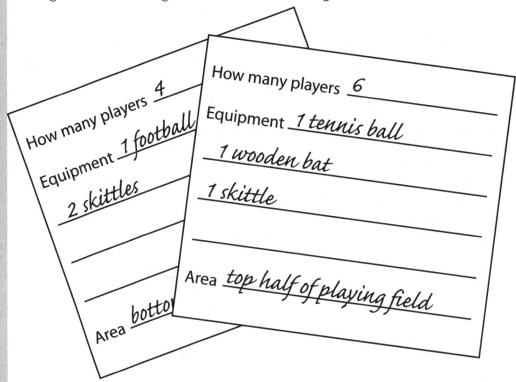

CREATING A GAME

RESOURCES AND CLASS MANAGEMENT

You will need a variety of equipment available so that children have a choice of equipment with which to hit, throw or kick during the course of their game and a further choice of equipment to use as a target area or goal posts. The children will also need sets of different coloured bands to wear in order to differentiate the various teams. Each group of players will need one of the pre-prepared cards (blank cards are provided on photocopiable page 63) on which they will find written the equipment to be used, the numbers of children in each group and the area in which they must play. You will also need a whistle and copies of photocopiable page 62 for each group.

WHAT TO DO

Make sure that you begin the lesson with several of the warm-up activities so that all the children are fully prepared to play a game.

Tell the children to group themselves with their information card and give them a few minutes to decide:
■ how a goal is to be scored
■ how the equipment will be used to make the ball travel
■ no more than three rules for the game
■ how the group is to be split into teams.

It may be appropriate at this stage for children to use photocopiable page 62 to help them with this.

When you are satisfied that the groups have made their decisions, tell each group to number their players '1', '2', '3' and so on. Ask number 1 to go and collect the equipment they need for scoring a goal, ask number 2 to collect the remainder of the equipment needed by the group and ask number 3 to collect the appropriate number of coloured bands. Tell the children to go to the area you have allocated them and set up the equipment. At this point you may nominate one player from each group to act as umpire or referee as well as playing the game so that the games can operate fairly without your presence all the time. Tell the children that on your whistle they may begin their game.

NOW OR LATER

■ After the children have had a few minutes to settle into the game it may become apparent in some groups that clarification is needed regarding either rules or scoring of goals. Encourage children to resolve these by discussion if possible. Decide on which teaching point you will concentrate and move around each group encouraging, praising and coaching to one main teaching point, such as: good use of all the space; throwing or kicking with the correct technique; or flexible passing amongst players.

■ Towards the end of the lesson tell the children to return the equipment and come up and stand in a group with you. Ask each group for the results of their game and praise and encourage when they tell you.

■ Finally make sure all the children do a cooling-down activity so that they are prepared for more sedentary work indoors.

OBJECTIVES

To enable children to:
■ practise skills learned in skill sessions
■ work co-operatively
■ create their own rules.

CROSS-CURRICULAR LINKS

PSHE
Working co-operatively in teams.

ENGLISH
Instructional writing.

My warm-up chart

Write down two activities to warm up each body part before you take part in physical activity. Some should be done on the spot, some should be done on the move.

Name of body part	Activity 1	Activity 2
Legs		
Shoulders		
Hands		
Lungs		
Arms		
Trunk		

My progress chart 1 – Invasion games

Activity	Number of repetitions	Date	Number of repetitions	Date	Number of repetitions	Date
Catching a large ball						
Catching a small ball						
Scoring a goal						
Hitting a target with a ball						
Bouncing a large ball						
Bouncing a small ball						
Dribbling a ball in a figure of eight						

My progress chart 2 –
Striking and fielding games

Activity	Number of repetitions	Date	Number of repetitions	Date	Number of repetitions	Date
Bowling a ball underarm						
Hitting a ball with a bat						
Scoring a rounder or a run						
Stumping a wicket or post						
Catching a small ball						
Retrieving a ball						
Hitting a target with a ball						

Name   Date

My progress chart 3 – Net and wall games

Activity	Number of repetitions	Date	Number of repetitions	Date	Number of repetitions	Date
Hitting a ball with a hand						
Catching a ball from a rebound						
Hitting a ball over a net						
Throwing and catching a ball over a net						
Throwing and catching a ball against a wall						
Using a backhand stroke						
Hitting a ball with a bat/ racket						

Name   Date

My fitness record

■ Choose three different activities like running, skipping, or playing a ball game to do for one minute without stopping.

■ Find your pulse on your wrist and count the number of heartbeats you feel in 20 seconds. You may need to ask your teacher to show you how to take your pulse.

■ Multiply the number of heartbeats after 20 seconds by three and write it down in the table below.

■ When you have finished, take your pulse rate again. How long does it take for your pulse rate to be the same as it was before you began?

Name of activity	Pulse rate after 20 seconds	Multiply by 3	Time pulse takes to return to normal

Name of activity	Pulse rate after 20 seconds	Multiply by 3	Time pulse takes to return to normal

Name of activity	Pulse rate after 20 seconds	Multiply by 3	Time pulse takes to return to normal

Food for fitness

On the plates below draw some foods which you think will keep your body healthy and give you energy.

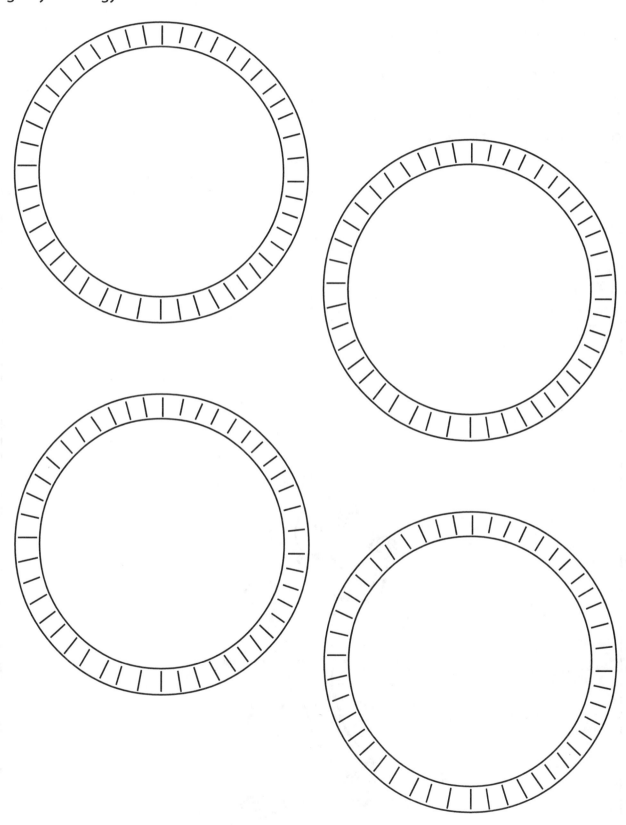

How should I behave?

Read these sentences and decide whether they are good actions or bad actions. Write them under the correct headings below.

1 Kim dodged away from her partner.
2 Imran kicked his partner's leg.
3 Richard dribbled the ball down the field
4 Samantha pushed a girl on the opposing team.
5 Jemma snatched the ball from Sumitra.
6 Raj threw the ball to Paul.

Good actions	Bad actions

Circle the mistakes

Physical Phil is about to hit the ball in his PE lesson. Can you find five mistakes and put a circle around each one?

Now write a sentence to explain each mistake.

1 _____

2 _____

3 _____

4 _____

5 _____

Creating a game

■ Group yourselves with your information card and between you decide what kind of game you are going to play.

What is the game called?	
How will a goal be scored?	Three rules for the game: 1 2 3
What will be your playing area?	How will the winning team be decided?

Ready to go! IDEAS FOR PE GAMES

Cards for creative games

How many players _____

Equipment _____

_____

_____

_____

Area _____

How many players _____

Equipment _____

_____

_____

_____

Area _____

How many players _____

Equipment _____

_____

_____

_____

Area _____

How many players _____

Equipment _____

_____

_____

_____

Area _____

How many players _____

Equipment _____

_____

_____

_____

Area _____

How many players _____

Equipment _____

_____

_____

_____

Area _____

Skills Grid — NATIONAL STANDARDS FOR KEY SKILLS

SKILLS		Page	Underarm throwing	Overarm throwing	Rolling a ball	Catching	Hitting a ball	Retrieving a ball	Kicking a ball	Dodging and feinting	Using the space	Bouncing a ball	Aiming
Section 1 – Warm-up activities	Whistle and run	9									✔		
	Roll and snatch	10			✔			✔					
	Left and right bounce	10										✔	
	Follow my leader change	11									✔		
	Body bounce	12									✔		
	Count and throw	13		✔		✔							
	Touch home	14									✔		
	Up and down	14	✔			✔							
	Lose your partner	15								✔			
	Two ball catch	16		✔		✔							
Section 2 – Invasion games	Dribble me round	17							✔		✔		
	Dodge duo	18								✔			
	Dribble and push	19					✔						
	Block the ball	20							✔	✔			
	Throw and bounce	20		✔		✔						✔	
	Shoot and throw	21		✔				✔					✔
	Chest pass shuttle	22		✔		✔						✔	
	Spot your number	23	✔			✔							
	Long run throwing	24		✔		✔	✔		✔				
	Pass, dribble and shoot	25							✔				✔
	Piggy in the middle	25		✔								✔	✔
	Escape your partner	26		✔		✔				✔	✔		
Section 3 – Striking/fielding games	Bowl and bat	28	✔				✔						✔
	Knock the skittle	29	✔		✔			✔					✔
	Roll, snatch and throw	29	✔		✔			✔					
	Hoop bounce	30			✔			✔				✔	✔
	Throw and run	31		✔				✔			✔		
	Hit, bounce, hit	32					✔						
	Three star batting	33	✔				✔	✔					
	Touch skittle	34	✔	✔									
	Base touch	35	✔				✔	✔					
	Ball snatch	36			✔			✔					✔
	Counting shuttle	37	✔			✔							
	Three versus three	38	✔				✔	✔			✔		
Section 4 – Net/wall games	Back and front bouncing	39					✔						
	Aim the hit	40					✔					✔	✔
	To and fro	40	✔				✔						✔
	High and low throwing	41	✔			✔							✔
	Side by side batting	42					✔						
	Hit and catch	43				✔	✔						
	Trio catching	44				✔							✔
	Batting challenge	45					✔						
	Wall tennis	46					✔				✔		✔
	Catch me	47	✔			✔							
	1, 2, 3, throw	48	✔			✔						✔	
	Backhand bounce	48					✔						
Section 5 Mini-games	Playing a mini-game	51	✔	✔		✔	✔	✔	✔	✔	✔	✔	✔
	Creating a game	53	✔	✔	✔	✔	✔	✔	✔	✔	✔	✔	✔